Fantasy Football for Smart People

25 Mysteries Solved to Help You

Draft a Better Team

Jonathan Bales, Founder of RotoAcademy

D1057513

Fantasy Football for Smart People
25 Mysteries Solved to Help You Draft a Better Team

Table of Contents

Fantasy Football for Smart People: 25 Mysteries Solved to Help You Draft a Better Team tackles some of fantasy football's most vital questions to see which beliefs are dogmatic and which stand up to scrutiny.

Postface

Preface

This *Fantasy Football for Smart People* series has been so much fun to write, but it's just getting started. I'm adding five new titles to the book series this year, all of which are going to help you dominate either season-long leagues or daily fantasy football.

The first book I wrote in a style similar to this one—as a collection of essays—is now the top fantasy football book on Amazon. I use such a format because 1) I think it's the most appropriate way to tackle in-depth topics and 2) much of my content is about answering fantasy football's most pressing questions or rejecting "established" truths, and the each-chapter-is-its-own-idea format lends itself nicely to that structure.

Fantasy Football for Smart People: 25 Mysteries Solved to Help You Draft a Better Team is composed of 25 separate questions whose I answers I believe can have a serious impact on the way we approach the game. I do my best to provide those answers—or at least to deepen the discussion and promote critical thinking that is the backbone of any effective approach to fantasy football.

This is my first year as a true full-time fantasy sports writer, so I've had a lot of time to research and write. Thus, I've published a shitload of stuff this year to help you kick ass in your leagues. You can buy my other books on Amazon or at FantasyFootballDrafting.com.

I'll be hawking my draft guide again this year—complete with projections, rankings, sleepers, and more. I'll also selling an in-season guide with weekly projections and values for daily fantasy sites like DraftKings. I started that last season and it became way more popular than I envisioned, so it will be back and better than ever this season. It's all at FantasyFootballDrafting.com.

But the biggest news of the year is that I started a fantasy football school called RotoAcademy.com. For just a few bucks per month, RotoAcademy will deliver you year-round, book-length (yes, book-length) fantasy football analysis. I write the majority of the content—provided via monthly newsletters sent right to your email—but there are a few other really talented instructors as well. I personally promise that it will make you a significantly better fantasy owner, or I'll give you your money back.

Thanks for your support, and best of luck this season!

Some Free Fantasy Football Stuff for You

I like giving things away, so here's some stuff for you. The first is 10 percent off anything you purchase on my site—all books, all rankings, all draft packages, and even past issues of RotoAcademy. Just go to FantasyFootballDrafting.com and use the code "Smart10" at checkout to get the savings.

The second freebie is an entire issue of RotoAcademy. Why an entire issue for free? Because I'm really excited about this product and I think if you start reading, you'll be hooked and become a full-time student. Remember, this is a year-long training course that's absolutely guaranteed to turn you into a dominant fantasy owner.

Go to FantasyFootballDrafting.com for your free issue (RotoAcademy Issue II), add the item to your cart, and enter "RA100" at checkout to get it free of charge.

Finally, I've partnered with DraftKings to give you a 100 percent deposit bonus when you sign up there. Deposit $500 and then bam! you got $1,000. DraftKings is the main site where I play daily fantasy football. Deposit there through one of my links (or use https://www.draftkings.com/r/Bales) to get the bonus, use the "Smart10" code to buy my in-season package at FantasyFootballDrafting.com (complete with DraftKings values all year long), and start cashing in on your hobby.

A whole lot of readers profited last year, with one cashing $25,000 in *multiple* leagues since purchasing my in-season package. There's an outstanding investment opportunity in daily fantasy sports right now, and there's really no reason for you *not* to get involved.

1 How can I dramatically improve my team without a second of research?

Fantasy football is changing. With position rankings becoming more and more efficient, there's less opportunity to beat out opponents based on superior football knowledge alone. Even in casual fantasy leagues, the typical owner knows pretty much about football—far more than the average fan of any other sport—and I'd bet that the median fantasy football owner is of a true intermediate skill level rather than a beginner.

Much of this is due to people like me. Not that there aren't better fantasy owners out there than me—there are—but there's a wealth of really good content available to anyone willing to pay a few bucks (the free stuff ain't all that hot).

While understanding the specifics of each player each year is important, the best fantasy owners no longer beat others by outsmarting them in regards to player projections. The majority of player projections are more or less the same. I typically take a contrarian approach to projections and rankings, so mine can differ from the norm a bit more than most, but I'm probably an outlier.

Even my projections, which I'm biased toward since, you know, I make them, don't differ from the consensus like they used to. Only a few years ago, I used to have a pretty sizeable number of players ranked wildly above or below their ADP every single season. Now, not so much. The general public has caught up some.

That means that elite fantasy owners win by emphasizing certain position combinations and player types. I care less about the exact players I take and more about which types of players—big wide receivers, fast running backs who catch passes, and so on—as well as the position order. Is it best to draft three running backs in a row? Should we emphasize consistency in the early rounds? When is the best time to draft a quarterback? Such questions have now become more important than "How many touchdowns will Matt Ryan throw this year?"

Knowing What We Don't Know

Winning fantasy football leagues used to be like shooting fish in a barrel (and by that I mean it was easy, although that idiom seems like it might be quite difficult in practice). You used to be able to inflict damage on opponents solely with superior player knowledge.

The biggest change in fantasy football that I've seen in the past few years is that, whereas it used to be about what you know, now it's about understanding what you *don't* know and acting accordingly. I truly believe that the biggest step you can take in fantasy football is realizing that you probably aren't as good as you think you are.

It's not just you, though. By and large, we aren't very good at making season-long or weekly fantasy football projections. It's just really difficult.

But you can acquire an advantage by *knowing* that you don't know. Accounting for your own fallibility as an owner is vital. Two examples.

First, I'm a big believer in a "wisdom of the crowd" approach to drafting. While I don't think you should blindly copy expert rankings, you should at least consider other points of view. If you have a player ranked No. 20

but his average draft position is No. 3, you better be damn sure you know something others don't.

If you think about it, it's pretty obvious that the crowd matters. Who do you think is ranked more accurately: a player ranked No. 20 overall with an ADP of No. 3, or one ranked No. 20 overall with the same No. 20 overall ADP? When experts have a consensus opinion that matches your opinion, it strengthens that belief.

Second example. I play daily fantasy football on sites like DraftKings, where players are given a fake salary and you need to create a team within the confines of a salary cap. The league ends after just one week's worth of games, and there's a whole lot of variance involved with that. There's skill, too, but for the most part, I believe those playing fantasy football are way worse at projecting players from week to week than what they think.

Even if you assume week-to-week fantasy production is completely random (which it's not), you can actually still win fantasy football. The reason is that you're competing with other humans, most of whom aren't accounting for said randomness.

Much of my daily fantasy football strategy revolves around targeting certain player types (similar to what I do in season-long leagues), preferably those coming off of a poor performance or two. Typically, those players drop in salary. People overreact to a small sample of events, mistaking noise for a signal, and bypass those "struggling" players. In effect, they're buying high on players who are "hot" with the thinking that they can accurately predict events that, while not totally random, are filled with uncertainty.

The point: you can be very successful in random or mostly random environments by going against the grain.

Maximizing Your Bullets

In my daily fantasy football example, my strategy is more or less to locate production at its cheapest possible point. So if I like wide receiver X at $8,000, I'll see how easily I can replace that production with a cheaper player, normally by targeting those who have underachieved lately, thus offering long-term production at a price that represents faux short-term struggles. In almost every case, cheaper equals better because it allows for flexibility elsewhere.

Well, the same is true in season-long fantasy football. When possible, you want to identify the cheapest possible price you can pay for certain levels of production. You could argue that Zac Stacy circa his 2013 rookie year was a very close approximation of Doug Martin, for example. Martin was a top three pick in every draft, however, while Stacy was drafted after the 10th round. Much of that had to do with projected workload, but take a look at their measurables and college stats:

Zac Stacy: 5-9, 216 pounds, 3,143 yards, 5.4 YPC, 4.55 40-yard dash, 6.70 three-cone drill, 4.17 short shuttle, 27 reps

Doug Martin: 5-9, 215 pounds, 3,431 yards, 5.6 YPC, 4.55 40-yard dash, 6.79 three-cone drill, 4.16 short shuttle, 28 reps

Stacy is Finkle! Finkle is Martin! Martin is Einhorn! Wait, what?

Stacy is basically the exact same player as Martin, which isn't a positive for the Tampa Bay Bucs. They could have saved the first-round pick they spent on Martin and acquired the same player four rounds later. But YAY SCOUTING!

For fantasy purposes, Stacy was a very close Martin approximation who could be had for almost nothing.

But cheaper isn't better in fantasy football if you aren't *rewarded* for spending less. In daily fantasy, you acquire more cap space when you pick cheaper players. In season-long, the benefit of willingly cashing in a draft pick for a lower one is. . .more draft picks!

Now I know that some of you play online in leagues that don't allow pre-draft or in-draft trades. SUX2BU. But with dynasty and keeper leagues growing and online fantasy draft software improving, the majority of fantasy owners can do one simple thing to increase their chances of taking home the crown: trade back and get more picks.

Before diving into the value of trading back in fantasy drafts, I want to look at how it's worked out for NFL teams. There's a really good article on the topic over at rotoViz, with this image showing the number of draft picks for teams over the past 15 years.

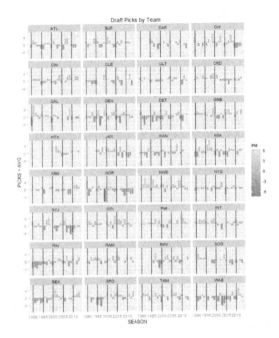

Draft Picks by Team

The Patriots, Packers, and Steelers have had the most picks over the timeframe, and you could argue they've also seen the most long-term success of any franchises. The Eagles also rank near the top, and they've surely been the most successful team to not win a championship.

Meanwhile, the Redskins, Lions, and Raiders rank at the bottom of the list in terms of total draft picks. No surprise that they've been among the least successful teams on the field.

The best NFL teams are usually those that draft the best. But drafting "best" might be less about hitting on a higher-than-average percentage of picks and more about maximizing the total picks. In a highly random environment, we'd expect the best long-term performers to be those that maximize opportunities.

We see this in a variety of fields; you can't improve the degree of your luck per se—it will always regress toward the mean over the long run—but you can certainly improve the *probability* that you experience good luck by maximizing opportunities.

If the NFL draft were primarily about picking more efficiently than other teams, we wouldn't see such a strong correlation between drafting success and pick volume. The best teams seem to understand that they probably aren't *that* much better than others at identifying talent, so the biggest advantage they can acquire is to bring in more players to maximize the odds of hitting on one.

Similarly, since fantasy football drafts have become more efficient—and thus more random—your biggest advantage probably doesn't lie in out-projecting your opponents. It comes in understanding your own fallibility and racking up opportunities (in the form of draft picks) to overcome it.

Quick and Easy

As fantasy owners, we should be looking for quick and easy ways to increase our win probability. When it comes to trading back in drafts, the return on your time is unimaginably larger than it is in regards to projecting players and creating a big board. The latter task isn't useless, but it requires a lot of time to create a rather small advantage.

We should be looking for just the opposite: actions that require little time but can allow for massive advantages. Normally, those actions are "big picture" concepts like accruing draft picks, drafting certain player types, and so on, as opposed to very detailed information like "Why do I have Josh Gordon projected three points ahead of Dez Bryant?"

Also notice that when we focus on specifics, the result is (usually) more fragile. I'll have a lot more to say about fragility, but we want to avoid draft strategies that are highly susceptible to destruction from variance. If I alter a player's projection by 100 yards, it can drastically change his place in my rankings. That's fragile. It's best to avoid processes that are influenced heavily by randomness, often requiring a whole lot of work for minimal reward and the potential for big-time chaos, in favor of processes and actions that won't be affected by chaos, or could even benefit from it.

In many ways, loading up on draft picks is an action that indeed benefits from randomness. In effect, you're saying, "Well I don't really know as much as I think we know about these players, so I want to get as many of them as I can, as cheaply as possible, to maximize the probability of hitting." When there's a whole lot of randomness in a season, top picks tend to have less production than expected and the value of trading down soars.

A (Simple) Fantasy Football Trade Value Chart

NFL teams have a trade value chart (which is completely off, by the way), so they all more or less have a set level of compensation required for each pick. Fantasy owners have no such chart, so it's basically like the Wild West on draft day. If my Uncle Bruce asks me if I want to trade Josh Gordon for a 14th-round pick one more time, I swear I'm shutting down the league.

Because of that, every trade really needs to be taken on a case-by-case basis based on a number of factors. Nonetheless, I've done some research on historic fantasy draft pick value to establish some sort of baseline trade value chart.

That's a really difficult task, though, because how do we define a player's value? We can look at consistency, or the probability of hitting on a specific pick, but that ignores the degree to which a pick could surpass a particular projection. Both the first and second overall selections might have, say, an 80 percent chance of hitting, but that would be rather trivial if the top overall pick has a much higher probability of outscoring every player by a wide margin.

We can use VBD—the points each pick typically scores over a replacement player at his position—but that ignores consistency. Thus, I've combined the two, charting the historic fantasy value of the top 24 picks based on their chances of hitting (consistency) and their scarcity (VBD). Why only the top 24? Because it's a lot of research and I only have ALL DAY LONG to work on this.

I started the process of making the chart using historic VBD calculations (the points each player scored over a baseline talent at his position). That was simple enough, but the problem is that you can't just plug in that data to create a value chart because, well, it doesn't work like that. It's much more valuable to have one player projected to score 400 points than it is to have two projected to score 200 points.

To translate VBD into a workable chart, I decided to look back at my past work on consistency in relation to draft slots. I think it's important to know historic success rates for each draft pick because it should have significant implications on the draft chart. If you could expect to hit a home run with the No. 1 overall pick 95 percent of the time, for example, that would drastically alter the value of the selection. So I charted the value of the top 24 picks in terms of VBD and a combination of total points and consistency.

For the record, by 'consistency' I mean the regularity with which owners have been able to hit on players. I constituted a 'hit' as a player who scored at least 70 percent of the total points of the No. 1 player at his position.

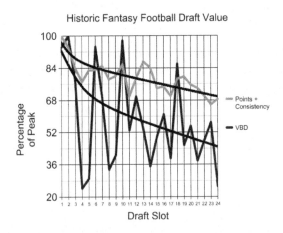

Historic Fantasy Football Draft Value

So what does this tell us? Well, it means that the drop in draft pick value isn't quite as dramatic as VBD makes it out to be. In reality, a late-first round pick hits just about as often as a mid-first, so there shouldn't be a huge drop in value on our chart after the first few selections.

Using that data, I was able to create an initial fantasy football trade value chart for the first two rounds in a 12-man league.

Fantasy Football Draft Value

When analyzing both consistency and scarcity, late-second-round picks have historically been worth right around half of the No. 1 overall selection. This chart accounts for that.

Also note the steep drop in the first five or six picks. That represents the fact that there have typically been about that many truly elite "can't-miss" prospects in fantasy drafts. Sometimes it's a little more, sometimes a little less, but there's definitely extra value in being able to nab one of those players. To give you an idea of how much value there is at the top of the draft, consider that the drop from the first overall pick to the second is the same as that from No. 16 to No. 24.

So what does this tell us about how we should act in fantasy drafts? I think the most obvious conclusion is that there's not a dramatic difference between picks between the late-first round and late-second round. If you're picking in the top five, you'd need a handsome return—maybe two second-round picks—in order to move back. But if you're picking in the late-first and an elite player doesn't fall to you, strongly consider moving back and picking up extra selections. The value of "maximizing your bullets" probably exceeds any additional consistency/scarcity that pick can offer you over a second-rounder.

A Robust Approach to Position Uncertainty

Whether or not you load up on draft picks, you can use the same theory that suggests you should stockpile selections—that the most effective way to enhance results in a mostly random environment is to increase opportunities—to determine the best course of action in terms of *which* positions to select.

In effect, there's an inverse relationship between uncertainty and the value of more opportunities. If you were a perfect dart thrower, you wouldn't need more than one dart in order to hit a bullseye. The extra opportunities have no value in an environment of perfect skill.

As we introduce variance into the equation, though, the value of extra chances increases. The worse you are at darts, the more value each extra dart throw would have to you.

In the same way, the more uncertainty and scarcity inherent to a certain position, the more "darts" you should throw at it. I've done a lot of position consistency research in the past that suggests quarterback is by far the easiest position to predict, both on the season-long and weekly levels. They have the largest sample size of relevant plays and the elite players at the position tend to remain elite.

Meanwhile, think about the randomness involved with a position like running back. First, they get hurt. A lot. If you drafted Doug Martin or Arian Foster in 2013, you probably had a hell of a time fighting your way into the playoffs.

Second, they're highly dependent on usage for production. That makes certain guys predictable—namely, the ones who see a high number of touches. But once you get past the ninth or tenth round of fantasy drafts, you're typically taking players who aren't starters and/or see few touches, so you're basically banking on a starter getting hurt for your pick to be worthwhile. Good luck predicting injuries.

Since mid and late-round running back production is basically a crapshoot, the goal should be to "throw shit at the wall and see what sticks." You can and should still select the right types of running backs—blazing fast, heavy if possible, pass-catchers, etc—but in a highly uncertain environment, it's just a numbers game.

Also note that you always need position scarcity for a position to be of value. Kicker performance is very random, too, but they have little value since there's not much scarcity at the position, meaning the top performer won't be that much better than a replacement player.

It's not really groundbreaking to suggest you should draft more running backs than quarterbacks, but you should also draft a higher number relative to your starting requirements. If you start one quarterback, for example, you might draft two of them—double the starting requirements. Even if you start three running backs, though, you should draft far more than double that number (assuming roster space allows for it), loading up particularly in the middle and late rounds as the draft becomes more random. In most leagues, I'd prefer two quarterbacks (at most, and sometimes just one), one tight end, kicker, and defense, and the rest running backs and wide receivers.

If you made it to the end of this 3,000-word rant on stockpiling fantasy football draft picks, you're probably an absolutely maniacal fantasy football psychopath. Never change.

2 Do players tank after signing big contracts?

I like money. I write for a few different reasons, but if we're being honest, the strongest is probably that it helps me make money. And the more money I can make, the more incentivized I am to do a really good job.

I'm going to guess that you also like money. And regardless of where we stand on the more complicated topic of how much money can increase our happiness, I don't think that I'd be going out on too much of a limb in predicting that you're also motivated, at least in part, to make more money.

Well, football players are the same way. Even though they all make well above the median household income from the moment they enter the NFL, it's not like the majority of players are raking in millions and millions of dollars a year. So when they come into the NFL and get a little taste of that money, they presumably want more.

I've done some past analysis that suggests you shouldn't specifically target players in contract seasons. Quarterbacks, running backs, wide receivers, and tight ends have all performed roughly the same (slightly worse as a whole, actually) in the season prior to becoming a free agent than they did in the two seasons before the contract year. There are outliers in both directions, of course, but overall, players don't play much better than normal in contract seasons.

I don't think that's necessarily evidence that those players aren't motivated to obtain a new contract, but just that the motivation isn't any higher in the year right before a new deal than in previous seasons. If you're a third-round draft pick, you're probably playing your ass off from the moment you enter the league so that you can stay there. With the average NFL career somewhere in the range of three years, young players know they have a limited window to cash in.

When the Motivation Stops

It's your lucky day. Your boss just praised you and your value to the company, so much so that he's rewarding you with a five-year, $60 million contract extension. You never topped six figures in a year, so the jump in salary is ~~literally never going to happen~~ awesome.

With $12 million in the bank in the first year, are you going to be as motivated to perform as you were when you were struggling to get a promotion? Be honest with yourself. You might come out of the extension on fire to prove to your boss that he made the right call, but eventually that motivation will dissipate.

Then you'll just be stuck there at a job you really don't like, wishing you could leave to go play with your millions of dollars, with zero motivation to help the company grow. Well, that's the position I'd be in, anyway. If I suddenly had $12 million in the bank, I can promise you the quality of my writing would deteriorate in a hurry.

Does that mean I don't take much pride in what I do? Yeah, maybe, I don't know. But that's what would happen, and I suspect the same lack of motivation would also strike a lot of young NFL players. Anecdotally, I've always thought that certain types of players—the ones who are motivated to play more for monetary gains than to truly improve their craft—rarely seem to provide their teams with a return on their investment.

But I didn't know for sure, so I ran some numbers.

The Numbers on the Post-Contract Downfall

To test this theory, I researched the current largest contracts in terms of guaranteed money. I sorted them by position, analyzing just over five dozen players in total. I charted their average fantasy rank (at their position) in the two years prior to their massive contract extensions versus (when applicable) their average fantasy rank in the two years afterward.

Quarterbacks

Here are the quarterbacks I studied. The smaller the bar, the better the ranking.

The biggest drop in play came from Mark Sanchez, although he should have never been given a contract extension in the first place. Overall, there certainly appears to be an effect here.

Of the quarterbacks I analyzed, the average drop in fantasy rank was 3.5 spots. While that might seem insignificant, it's actually 38.0 percent of their pre-contract rank.

Running Backs

If I were an NFL GM, I don't think I would ever give a running back a contract extension. Running backs are so dependent on the offensive line for production and possess such a sad-looking career trajectory—I've shown that running backs enter the NFL at peak efficiency and slowly decline from there—that it just doesn't make sense to pay them.

But some teams do just that. Because what could go wrong when you forgo science/math in favor of dogma? Nothing, nothing at all.

So what happens when running backs get huge contracts with lots of guaranteed money?

At the top of the guaranteed money spectrum, we see a few backs who have really failed to live up to expectations in DeAngelo Williams and Arian Foster. Even the backs near the lower end—Jonathan Stewart and Michael Bush among them—have failed to live up to their deals.

If there's one contract on this list that made sense, however, it was that for Jamaal Charles. When he signed an extension with the Chiefs in 2010, Charles was still just 24 years old. He was coming off of a decent-but-not-spectacular season in which he ran for 1,120 yards, hauled in 40 catches for 297 yards, and scored eight total touchdowns.

At the time, though, Kansas City saw enough of Charles, who displayed all of the predictors of success for running backs—youth, speed, pass-catching ability, and rushing efficiency. The Chiefs got an absolute steal on Charles with a six-year, $28 million deal. Imagine if they waited a year, after which Charles rushed for nearly 1,500 yards and unbelievably averaged 6.4 YPC.

Charles is an exception. Overall, the results haven't been pretty for running backs after signing big deals.

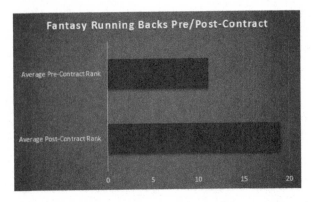

The running backs I studied finished with an average rank of 11.1 in the seasons before their contract extensions, but only 19.0 following the deals. That's a drop of 71.2 percent.

Wide Receivers

When I decided to do this analysis, it was because of a handful of players who I could recall signing hefty contracts, then proceeding to apparently pack it in. I didn't really think about it at the time, but all of those players—Larry Fitzgerald, Mike Wallace, Marques Colston, Miles Austin, and Victor Cruz, among others—were wide receivers.

It could just be variance, of course, but the data sure does seem to point to wide receivers playing much, much worse post-contract.

You can see quite a few "after contract" bars extend above those for "before contract," meaning the top-paid wide receivers haven't done much as a group to live up to their deals. Brandon Marshall made the largest improvement, jumping from an average rank of 18.5 to 7.5, but part of that was probably due to being reunited with Jay Cutler in Chicago.

Take a look at the overall drop. Note that I removed Calvin Johnson from this set of data because he had an average fantasy rank of 1.0 in the two years prior to his big contract extension, i.e. there was no room for improvement. I'll discuss that idea in a bit.

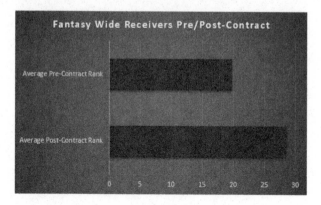

The group of wide receivers dropped from an average rank of 19.7 all the way down to 28.5. That's a 47.1 percent decline.

Tight Ends

When I performed the study on players in contract years, tight end was the only position to actually see an increase in production over prior seasons (albeit a very modest one). I wrote it off as variance.

Now, I've found that although the tight ends as a whole see their fantasy rank drop after signing a big deal, it's the smallest effect of any position. Here are the individual tight ends I charted.

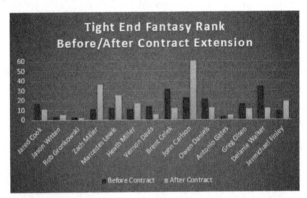

And overall. . .

The typical tight end dropped 1.5 spots after signing a new contract, constituting just a 9.9 percent decline from his pre-contract rank.

Combining all positions, the average pre-contract rank was 14.0 and the mean post-contract rank was 19.5. So if you were asked to predict the final fantasy rank of a random, unknown player who just signed a new deal, your best bet would be to go with around five to six spots lower than his average rank in the prior two seasons.

Failure Rates By Position

I used average ranks to give you an idea of how far players at each position have fallen post-contract, but an even better way to analyze them might be to just do a simple tally: what percentage of players at each position have dropped after receiving an extension?

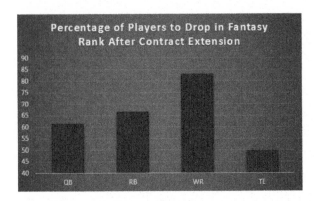

Analyzing each position in this manner, the inability of wide receivers to continue to dominate after signing a big deal is very apparent. It's significant when you consider the average pre-contract rank for all wide receivers (including Calvin Johnson) was 18.6.

So why is this the case? Could it just be randomness?

Perhaps, but my guess is that, at least for quarterbacks, the type of mentality that would lead to dominance at the position (at any point) would be one that could result in more sustainable success than that for wide receiver or running back.

It's not that running backs and wide receivers don't need to be committed to improving their games, but just that playing quarterback so clearly requires such an incredible combination of skill, determination, and preparedness— more so than at any other position, by far—that you just won't see the same sort of lack of consistency as you might at wide receiver.

Wide receivers can get lucky, happening upon a breakout campaign perhaps without an elite work ethic. I don't think that's the case at quarterback—the players who break out necessarily need to put in the time—and that approach lends itself better to 1) a lower bust rate and 2) more sustainable success.

And as for tight ends, well, I just don't know.

The Limitations

I want to briefly address the limitations of this analysis, of which there are at least a couple. The main one is that players who sign contract extensions are generally outliers; the reason they got a new deal is (usually) because they performed better-than-average.

Because of that, we'd expect players coming off of contract extensions to perform a little bit worse than they did previously *no matter what*. Coming off of an outlying season, their play would typically regress toward the mean regardless of their level of motivation.

There's also a limit on how highly a player can rank, while no such limit exists for downside. The reason I removed Calvin Johnson from the sample is because he couldn't possibly improve upon his first place average. I limited the impact of that effect by showing the probability of a player dropping at each position post-contract, but it's still an issue.

The final problem is that there aren't necessarily great parameters to know when we should expect a player to buck the trend and continue to perform at a high level even after signing a big fat deal. I broke the numbers down by position, but there's more work to be done there. Perhaps wide receivers of a certain age typically continue to perform well if they're seeking yet another deal in the future, for example.

Conclusions

However, I still think the data is actionable (even if it's only as a tiebreaker between two players). While the average fantasy ranks of the players before their extensions are outliers, it's not like they're incapable of being overcome. I don't think that the outlier theory is enough to make up for the incredible decline we see with post-contract wide receivers, for example. There really does appear to be a meaningful effect.

And even if we can't know for sure if a particular player will play at a high level, we never know that. All we can do is play the percentages, and the numbers say to avoid players who just signed big contract extensions if a comparable non-extension player is available.

Further, you can perhaps improve upon your ability to predict a decline in production by pairing the data with rumblings you hear about a player. When you see a new deal handed out to Player X who just had a single breakout season and is rumored to have a poor work ethic, it's a different situation from someone like Larry Fitzgerald, for example, who we pretty much know works his tail off.

3 Are small-school prospects better fantasy options than big-school players?

It seems like the impact of small-school players in the pros grows every season. Players like Vincent Jackson (Northern Colorado) and Marques Colston (Hofstra) have turned in dominant fantasy seasons, despite their humble college beginnings.

Intuitively, it makes sense that small-school prospects would be undervalued. As the overall talent level of college players grows, the gap between the big and small schools will shrink. That's primarily because the ground to gain for the elite college prospects is so much smaller than that for, say, DI-AA players, so the latter prospects have been able to "catch up." I also think the fact that NFL teams can find talent from any school has allowed talented high school athletes to attend smaller universities.

Whatever the reason, I've found some evidence in the past that small-school players are undervalued by NFL teams. However, I was interested in knowing if small-school skill position players have been superior to their big-school counterparts as fantasy producers.

The Numbers on Small-School Prospects

I decided to break up the data into two primary categories, sorting it by position and round. Since small-school players typically get drafted later, it wouldn't make sense to compare all small-school quarterbacks to all BCS quarterbacks, for example, because the latter group should be expected to produce at a higher level from their draft slot alone.

I'm more concerned with looking at, say, a third-round prospect and trying to figure out if his college can give us some insights into his potential NFL production. To grade that production, I used approximate value from Pro Football Reference, which is a pretty good catch-all metric that combines all relevant fantasy numbers.

Quarterbacks

Right off the bat, I found that BCS quarterbacks (those from the big conferences) have outperformed non-BCS quarterbacks, even after adjusting for draft round.

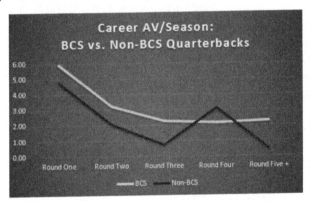

Outside of the fourth round, BCS quarterbacks have recorded better fantasy stats than non-BCS passers. The deviation from that trend is likely just due to variance.

First and second-round small-school quarterbacks have been particularly poor. Outside of a handful of names (Ben Roethlisberger Daunte Culpepper, and perhaps Joe Flacco and Alex Smith), most have been busts or mediocre at best: J.P Losman, David Carr, Patrick Ramsey, Kevin Kolb, John Beck, Shaun King, and Charlie Batch among them.

Note that Tony Romo (Eastern Illinois) wasn't included in this analysis because he went undrafted. His presence wouldn't significantly alter the results. The sample (which contains 156 quarterbacks over a 15-year period) is large enough to conclude that you probably want to favor BCS quarterbacks.

I think that big-school quarterbacks have found more NFL success for a few reasons. First, great quarterbacks are typically heavily recruited out of high school, so the best rarely sign with non-BCS schools.

Further, playing quarterback in the NFL seems to take a level of confidence that surpasses that required for every other position, and quarterbacks from schools like Alabama, Notre Dame, USC, Florida State, and so on seem like they're probably better equipped to deal with pressure and adversity. It's not that small-school quarterbacks can't be confident in their abilities—Joe Flacco has perhaps the most undeserved sense of arrogance I've ever witnessed, for example—but they aren't necessarily forced to deal with adversity on a consistent basis, so it can be difficult to determine if they have what I call "Goldilocks arrogance" (just enough to not care about what people say, but not so much that they fail to work hard).

Running Backs

If there's one position I thought would stand out in this analysis in favor of small-school options, it was running back. That's because running backs are so dependent on their offensive lines for production that it can become really difficult to grade them. We see that in the NFL, as running backs drafted in the third round or later have actually been *more* efficient than first and second-round backs since 2000. Wow. NFL scouts are typically a conceited bunch who throw out vague, meaningless buzzwords to display their intricate "knowledge" of how the game is played, but the truth is they have almost no clue what they're doing when it comes to running backs. The fact that the NFL draft is as inefficient as it is after all this time is a disgrace to the scientific process.

Moving on. Here's the data on BCS vs. non-BCS running backs.

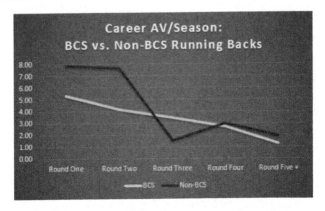

NFL teams have been horrible when it comes to drafting running backs in the early rounds. Among the first and second-round misses are Trent Richardson, Mark Ingram, Ryan Williams, Daniel Thomas, Jahvid Best, Toby Gerhart, Montario Hardesty, and Beanie Wells. There are others, too; that's just *what I can remember* from the past few drafts alone.

Meanwhile, there have been six non-BCS running backs drafted in the first two rounds since 1995: Ryan Mathews, Chris Johnson, LaDainian Tomlinson, DeAngelo Williams, Antowain Smith, and Matt Forte. Not all of those have been superstars, but L.T. is one of the most productive backs in NFL history and Smith is the only clear miss.

That's not a huge sample size and non-BCS running back success hasn't extended to later in the draft, but there's no clear BCS advantage as there is with quarterbacks.

Wide Receivers

Wide receiver is an interesting position because, up until very recently, most organizations were valuing the wrong traits in prospects. Whereas many teams still covet blazing-fast play-makers like Tavon Austin, it's the big, physical receivers who have been the most successful in the pros. Austin's value would absolutely soar if the NFL began awarding points for running horizontally across the field. If they stubbornly stick to their guns and force teams to actually get into the end zone to rack up points, though, players like Austin will be overvalued.

Such market inefficiencies can be exploited in the mid and late rounds, when shrewd teams acquire players who should have gone earlier for a cheaper price. A 6'3", 220-pound small-school prospect can make for an intriguing third-round pick, for example. Either way, here's the data on BCS vs. non-BCS wide receivers.

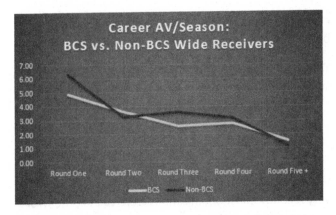

The non-BCS players have performed slightly better overall, but these lines are pretty similar. It's interesting to see another advantage for non-BCS first-rounders, which I think is the result of two things. First, first-round non-BCS receivers Randy Moss and Roddy White were pretty good I think, right? That helps. Second, NFL teams probably require a higher level of confidence to take a small-school prospect early in the draft. When a player like Moss is selected in the first round despite his off-field concerns and playing weak competition at Marshall, you know he's a stud.

Tight Ends

Finally, let's take a gander at the tight ends.

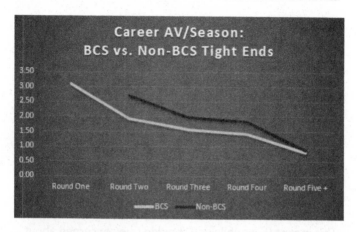

Interestingly, there have been no small-school tight ends taken in the first round since 1995. That's not completely surprising since the position was never really considered of incredible importance. In every other round, though, non-BCS tight ends have outperformed their big-school counterparts.

When you see a relatively small effect like the one with tight ends, you can't really be sure that it's meaningful. You can acquire more meaning when a bunch of small effects begin to add up, however, and I think that's what we're seeing with small-school running backs, wide receivers, and tight ends.

Whereas I believe there's good evidence to suggest that BCS quarterbacks should make for the best pros, that's not the case for BCS players at other positions. With the number of players in this study (over 1,000), the sample is large enough to conclude that non-BCS players at most positions appear to be undervalued. They aren't inherently better than big-school players, of course, but just better values when you consider the cost of drafting them.

When the School Matters

When an MLB player breaks out in his age-20 season with a .326 average, 30 home runs, and 83 RBI, you can pretty much bet he's going to be an outstanding pro. You can throw away how much time he spent in the minors or how much he got on base in college; with 162 games, one elite MLB season is a pretty significant sample size.

That's not the case in the NFL. Ten seasons of NFL data isn't as much as even a single MLB season, so there's a huge amount of variance inherent to most stats.

This means that, while you shouldn't be concerned about a player's college origins in his fifth NFL season, it can still have meaning a year or two into his career. When Matt Forte broke out in his rookie season, perhaps we should have had a little more confidence in his career path knowing that, coming from Tulane, he was perhaps undervalued (relative to other running backs). And maybe the opposite can be said of Felix Jones, who was highly efficient in his first two NFL seasons but never produced quality fantasy numbers, despite playing college ball in the SEC.

By no means do I think you should be selecting first and second-year players based solely on their school. But if you're in a dynasty draft or even if you're choosing between two rookies in a redraft league, keep in mind that NFL teams have typically been overly bullish on big-school names at every position other than quarterback.

4 Can college conference really predict NFL success?

I've been kind of fixated on this idea of analyzing NFL prospects based upon their college conference and, even more so, whether or not they attended a BCS school. I think people are pretty much in agreement that analyzing players in terms of small vs. big school has a lot of merit because 1) there's a clear difference between those players and 2) there's a large enough sample size of players to draw meaningful conclusions.

And indeed, there's some really strong evidence that there are conference-related inefficiencies to exploit in the draft. Those inefficiencies differ based on position; there are massive problems with the way that NFL teams draft running backs, for example.

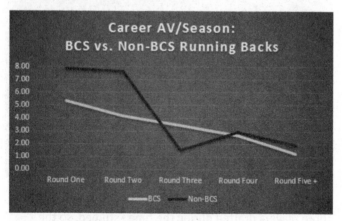

Because running back is such a difficult position to assess due to being so dependent on the offensive line, teams undervalue small-school talent; it also probably has something to do with them overlooking straight-line speed as a predictor of NFL success, and non-BCS players who gain a lot of notoriety can typically fly.

Anyway, analyzing by big/small school doesn't seem too controversial, does it? But a lot of people have trouble accepting that we should grade prospects based on the actual college conference. That's something I did at rotoViz, breaking down wide receivers based on conference.

One thing I did in that analysis was compare wide receiver production to what we'd expect based on where they were drafted. We'd naturally expect small-school receivers to have worse stats because they're drafted lower, but how do they perform relative to others drafted in their area?

Here's how things break down by conference. . .

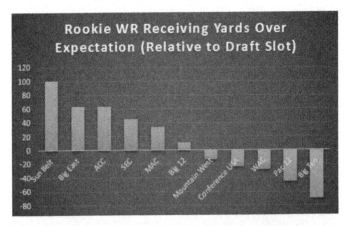

The Sun Belt checks in atop this list, but they had just three players drafted during the time I studied, so the numbers are just skewed by T.Y. Hilton. Otherwise, you can see that we don't see the same small-school success for wide receivers that we witness for backs.

But on the more micro level of actual conferences, we see that the Pac 12 and Big Ten have been absolutely awful at producing wide receiver talent. The Big Ten's ineptitude was actually what pushed me to do the analysis; to give you an idea of how bad they've been, consider that Arrelious Benn, Courtney Roby, and Charles Rogers rank among the top 10 in rookie receiving yards for Big Ten players drafted since 2000. Holy shit.

The Big Ten and Pac 12 rank at the bottom in terms of touchdowns, too.

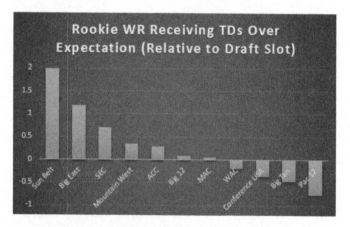

In terms of what we'd expect based on their draft slots, both Big Ten and Pac 12 receivers have been horrendous.

The question is whether or not this is meaningful or just a byproduct of randomness. Maybe I'm just interpreting something that's not there.

To answer that, let's go back to the two criteria that justifies analyzing on the macro level of conferences—a large sample and a clear difference between the prospects. As mentioned, there are some issues with sample size here for certain conferences, but those are primarily the small ones like the Sun Belt that have very few players drafted. Otherwise, we're talking about every receiver drafted since 2000, so the BCS conferences like the SEC and Big Ten have plenty of receivers in the sample.

But what about a clear difference between prospects? We have an obvious reason to think that small-school prospects will generally be worse than BCS players, but is there anything that differentiates, say, the Pac 12 from the ACC, such that we'd be justified in believing one produces a different type of prospect than the other?

I think there is.

Take a look at this.

Geography as Destiny

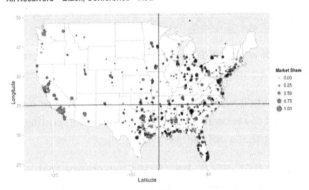

Conference

Pac-12 Conference

Hometown of College Football Wide Receivers

All Receivers = Black, Conference = Red

That's the hometown of Pac 12 wide receivers, as produced by the rotoViz "Geography as Destiny" app. The red areas are those of high density, and as you'd expect, they're nearly all out west where the colleges in the Pac 12 are located (with a lot in Texas, too, which produces top talent everywhere just because of the number of prospects).

Now let's compare that to the hometowns for Big Ten receivers.

Geography as Destiny

Conference

Big Ten Conference

Hometown of College Football Wide Receivers

All Receivers = Black, Conference = Red

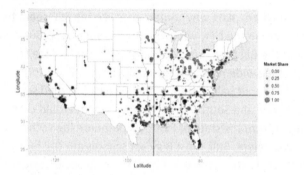

Shocker...almost no one from California or anywhere out west, almost no one down south, and nearly everyone from the Midwest and parts of the Northeast. Some top high school football prospects travel across the country to attend the school they desire, but most stay local. They have pressure from their friends and family to play for the "home school," and most probably want to just stay in the area anyway; it's close to home-cookin' and many are basically already legends in the area.

We can do this with any conference and any position, meaning we now have a very clear difference in the types of players who attend certain conferences. So can that explain the difference in wide receiver production at the NFL level?

My first hunch was that we'd see the southern-based conferences produce better talent because, since the players come from states like Texas, Florida, and Arizona, they just have more football under their belts; due to the weather, they can play year-round, which is a clear advantage over those players in states like New York and Pennsylvania who can play only six or seven months out of the year.

That might explain why conferences like the SEC seem to dominate in the NFL, while the Big Ten falls back. But what about the Big East—the top-ranked BCS conference for producing wide receivers since 2000? Well, don't forget that for about half that time, the Big East included schools like Miami and South Florida—colleges that would clearly benefit from the state of Florida's premiere high school football talent. Still, most Big East schools are still located up north. Further, the Pac 12 has been atrocious, and the majority of their schools are located in areas with warm-weather climates.

Another potential theory is that colleges in certain areas of the country are more inclined to play a certain style of football that might help or hinder players at certain positions. SEC schools are known for producing speed, for example, while the Big Ten is more "ground-and-pound" type of football. However, I actually think that would tend to help Big Ten receivers; the conference tends to emphasize size over speed, which is a positive for wide receivers. Further, with teams in the conference running the ball quite a bit, we might expect Big Ten receivers to drop too far in the draft, and thus offer value.

Yet another idea is that the cornerbacks in certain conferences, such as the Big Ten, might just be worse. Maybe students at high schools in the Northeast and Midwest are less likely to view cornerback as a "cool" position, with the top talent focusing on contributing on offense. That would allow Big Ten receivers to perform well against inferior opponents, vault up draft boards because of it, then disappoint in the pros once they face stiffer competition.

This is just me thinking this through and ultimately telling you I don't know why certain BCS conferences would produce better or worse talent than others. Are the coaches better? Do NFL teams overvalue certain conferences because of some sort of preconceived notions?

I still think there's something to the idea that certain areas of the country should naturally produce the best talent. My best guess is still that it's a combination of weather and overall competition, and since prospects tend to attend a nearby university, the conferences with schools located primarily in warm-weather areas will attract the best players and produce the top NFL talent.

There's more work to do here. Perhaps breaking things down by hometowns might help; if we see that the majority of Miami's recruits who are from Florida outplay those from out-of-state, for example, that could be evidence of the warm-weather effect.

But for now, because I want to leave you with a piece of information you can actually use, here you go: there's a massive advantage to be gained by seeking small-school running backs, but not one for receivers. While non-BCS backs are undervalued and often thrive in the pros, the wide receiver market is pretty much efficient in regards to school size, so focus more on weight and other underappreciated predictors of NFL wide receiver success.

5 How can I analyze past seasons to acquire future value?

Although there are still plenty of inefficiencies, fantasy football markets are at least becoming efficient enough that it's going to be difficult for you to out-project the expert consensus on individual players and consistently beat out ADP. You can still do it, but there are perhaps other more efficient ways to beat the crowd.

Most of the advanced strategies center around some form of a contrarian draft strategy—purposely going against the grain to generate value. You can't really go against the grain if you don't know what the consensus will be, though, so it's important to understand how the market will react to certain events.

One thing over which fantasy owners typically overreact is the previous season's stats. That's why I'm so big on studying semi-long-term trends. That doesn't necessarily have a ton of value on the individual level because players and situations change all the time, but it has a ton of value on the positional level; future fantasy point distributions for each position are more likely to resemble the average of the past five seasons than they are to resemble last season alone.

Quarterback

I use the example of 2012 fantasy drafts all the time because a bunch of quarterbacks were drafted unusually high due to their finish in 2011. If we studied five-year trends, though, we would have seen how much of an outlier 2011 really was for quarterbacks.

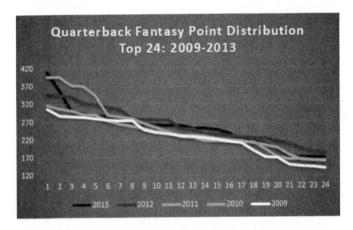

The elite passers in 2011—one through five—performed significantly higher than those in prior years. This was a pretty simple case of hey-guys-they-aren't-going-to-do-this-again—and you can see that in 2012 they didn't, as the quarterback curve flattened out—but fantasy owners still went nuts over quarterbacks in 2012.

The situation is even easier to see looking at just the top 12 passers.

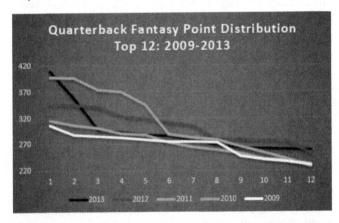

Peyton Manning's 2013 season was one of the best ever—more on that in a bit—but otherwise, no one was close to touching the top five passers from 2011. To give you an idea of how ridiculously they performed, consider that those five quarterbacks each posted more points than all but one quarterback in the prior six seasons.

Heading into 2012 fantasy drafts, shrewd owners knew that others were highly likely to overpay for those top quarterbacks. That would deflate their worth while also inflating the value at other positions. The value of going against the grain in that situation is pretty obvious; a contrarian strategy works because you're buying low on positions that perhaps underachieved in the previous season.

To give you an idea of how you might obtain value in a given season, let's examine the 2013 quarterback fantasy point distribution versus the five-year average.

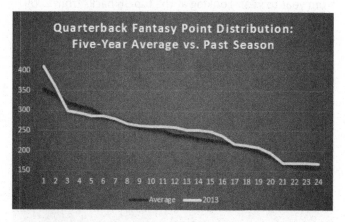

Right off the bat, you see that 2013 saw an immediate drop from the top, due solely to Manning's record-breaking year. Manning is a really unique player, but we'd never expect any quarterback to continue such dominance.

The rest of the 2013 quarterback distribution was fairly standard, but take a look at the elite passers after Manning. There's a bit of a drop there, and I think there's a great chance that those passers offer value in a lot of value in 2014 drafts.

Quarterbacks like Aaron Rodgers and Drew Brees were first-round picks just a couple years prior, but what's really changed since then? Nothing. They were over-drafted then, but owners have compensated too much. Until things change, I will be all over the elite quarterbacks who fall into the third and fourth rounds.

Running Back

The running back position has been remarkably consistent from year to year. Looking at the top 36 backs from 2009 to 2013, there's very little deviation from season to season.

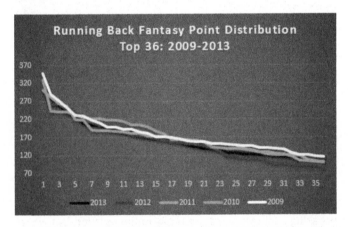

Note that one of the natural outcomes of analyzing point distributions is seeing the greatest fluctuations near the top. We're never going to see the No. 12 running back in

Year X differ from the No. 12 running back in Year X+1 by a crazy amount, but we might see the top running back's fantasy production really shift from one year to the next.

If you look at the running back who finished 12th in each of the past five seasons, for example, you see a high of 205 fantasy points (standard scoring) and a low of 177 fantasy points—a difference of 28 points. Meanwhile, the best No. 1 running back during that time checked in 48 points ahead of the worst No. 1 back.

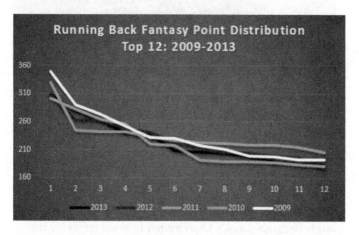

Looking at just the top 12 backs, you can see a deviation in the 2010 season; there was a really big drop from the top back, but then the production leveled out almost entirely from the No. 2 back to No. 12. The average drop from the No. 2 running back to No. 12 during the five years was 84 points with a high of 101; in 2010, it was just 38 points. In that situation, we'd need to be careful to realize that the 2011 running back distribution would be more likely to resemble long-term trends (with a greater slope) than the 2010 results—and you can see that happened.

The 2013 season was typical in just about every sense of the word for running backs as a whole.

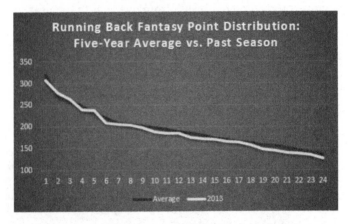

In my opinion, 2014 fantasy drafts will be about as efficient as they've been in a long time at the running back position, and the 2013 results are part of the reason.

Wide Receiver

The wide receiver position has been interesting to follow lately because there's been a clear upward trend for the position as a whole. While 100-yard rushing games have more or less remained constant over the past half-decade, the occurrence of 100-yard receiving games has increased by nearly 40 percent. Forty percent in five seasons!

After the WR1s, wide receiver fantasy production has been very constant from year to year.

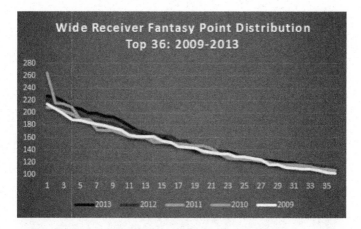

In the top 12 area, though, there have been some fluctuations.

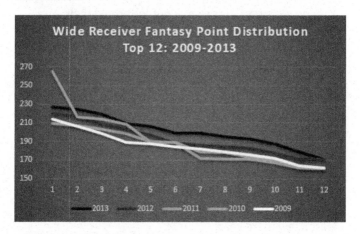

The clear outlier there is Calvin Johnson's 2011 season, which was simply out of this world. But the 2013 curve is also really interesting because it's leading the pack at nearly every spot. I don't think that's a fluke; we're not looking at a handful of spots rising and the rest achieving as normal, but rather a unified leap for all wide receivers.

Let's take a look at 2013 compared to the five-year average.

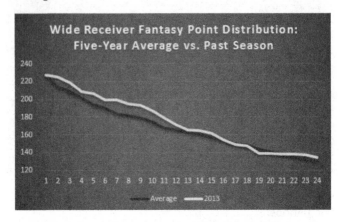

The top wide receivers clearly outperformed their projection in 2013, but I don't think they're going to regress in future years. The league is changing, and coaches are becoming more adept at using their No. 1 receivers—true big, physical, dominant No. 1s like Johnson, Josh Gordon, Dez Bryant, and so on.

The collective rise of wide receivers, particularly those near the top of boards, is why I'm so bullish on an early-receiver approach for certain owners—namely those with a late pick. I think there's really a good chance that the top 12 (or so) receivers continue to surpass expectations for at least a few more years.

Tight End

At the tight end position, it's all about outliers. Since the position is in the midst of a dramatic paradigm shift in the NFL, there are certain players who are far more fantasy-relevant than others; they're basically playing two different positions.

The recent popular consensus has been to either draft quarterbacks and tight ends early or wait completely and stream them off of waivers based on matchups. While I disagree that such a strategy is preferred for quarterbacks, I agree that it makes sense at tight end. If I miss out on an elite tight end, I probably won't draft one for a long time.

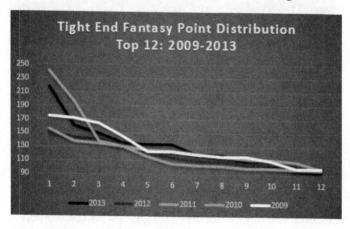

The steepness of some of those distributions represents the scarcity of players like Jimmy Graham. We don't see that sort of drop at other positions.

The problem is that we don't always see that scarcity. In 2011 and 2013, the top tight end was dominant. Here's 2013 compared to the five-year average.

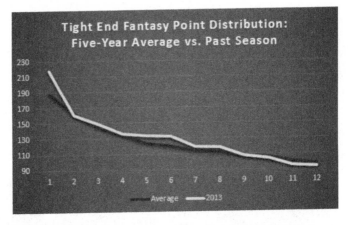

In 2009, 2010, and 2012, however, the distribution was pretty flat, i.e. using an early pick on a top tight end probably didn't pay off.

There are three reasons I'm still very much aboard the early-tight end train, though. First, we're still in the infancy of the shift in the offensive philosophy that's resulted in greater tight end usage, so the top options are still scarce.

Second, you have to hit on your tight end for the strategy to work, but that's true of any player. The chances of any first or second-round pick exceeding their ADP are minimal just because the cost is so high. And since tight ends actually have the highest year-to-year consistency of any position, a player like Graham has a better chance to dominate his position than any single running back, for example.

Finally, your goal is always to seek upside while maintaining as much of a floor as possible. With the potential that the elite tight ends offer to become outliers at the position, there's probably no safer way to acquire a high ceiling on your team.

6 What's the perfect fantasy football league?

I participate in too many fantasy leagues to mention without being horribly embarrassed, one of which is a league with some people work within the Dallas Cowboys organization (some writers, a Cowboys cheerleader, and a fan).

Now I'm not going to completely speculate on the quality of the owners in the league because some might be decent for all I know, but let me just say that Tom Brady was drafted in the first round. So there's that.

You'd think I could just run over a league like that. But after missing the playoffs last year, I'm currently 2-5 and in second-to-last place in the league. I've scored almost 50 points less than the cheerleader. I'm winning or in the top quarter of multiple high-stakes leagues, yet I can't crack the top half of a league in which Brady was a first-rounder and Jamaal Charles nearly slipped into the third.

You might argue that I'm writing this because I'm bitter, and you'd be exactly right. It's pretty annoying to make what you consider to be optimal decisions and then just get killed by a game filled with so much inherent variance.

So that's why I was glad to see Chris Liss's recent article on the increasing difficulty to win fantasy football. Here's the paragraph that struck me:

> There will always be luck in all fantasy sports, and more of it in football than anywhere else given the head-to-head set-up, the small sample and the way scoring depends so heavily on touchdowns. But the extent to which luck governs an activity should be inversely proportional to the amount of work it requires. I think recent developments are

adding much more work and only slightly more skill, and to the extent that there is more skill it's less about predicting true breakouts or handicapping team strength than digging into irrelevant minutiae like whether a slot receiver will catch six passes on a given day.

I couldn't agree more with that assessment. There's so much work that needs to be done to hold a competitive advantage over opponents, yet in most cases, that advantage won't even propel you to victory. In a 10-team league, I might own a 20 percent chance to win the championship. That's double the average owner, but I'd still need to participate in dozens of leagues to know for sure if my successes (or failures) are due to luck or skill. It's too much work for the miniscule potential returns.

That's one reason I'm moving more and more of my action to daily fantasy sports. Although there's obviously plenty of randomness involved there, too, I can at least participate in a large enough sample of leagues to see a return on my investment (of both money and time).

But I'll always participate in season-long leagues because, well, there's nothing quite like a preseason draft. The key is to figure out how we can minimize the randomness.

Deep Rosters/Starting Requirements

I was in a league last year that started 1 QB, 1 RB, 1 WR, 1 RB/WR, 1 TE, 1 K, and 1 D. That's the sort of league in which Demaryius Thomas is a flex play.

The smaller the rosters, the more inherent randomness. By expanding both rosters and starting lineup requirements, it will increase the amount of skill and knowledge needed to prosper. The Demaryius Thomas vs. Julio Jones decision is dictated more by luck than, say, Stephen Hill vs. Bryce Brown.

In my view, a deep league format like 1 QB, 3 RB, 5 WR, 2 TE, 1 QB/TE is suitable. That might seem freaking outrageous and it would certainly extend draft times, but it would also decrease the ability for crappy owners to win the championship.

Best-Ball Format

Chris mentioned that deep lineups can lead to difficult week-to-week matchup decisions that are governed primarily by luck, but that would disappear in a best-ball format. That means you don't choose starters each week; your top-scoring players are just automatically inserted into your lineup. If the goal is to increase the importance of the draft—the culmination of countless hours of research—over in-season moves, a best-ball format is the way to go.

All-Play + H2H

In Week 1, I scored 180-something points in a relatively thin league and I lost to the top scorer. I got a loss just the same as if I scored 50 points. That's not right.

My personal preference is to crown the total-points winner the champion at season's end, but many people enjoy the head-to-head nature of fantasy football when playing with friends and coworkers.

If you want to keep head-to-head matchups, at least add in an "all-play" element to that structure. In that format, you get a win or loss for your heads-up matchup and another win or loss for finishing in the top half or bottom half for the week. In an all-play league structure, I would have finished 1-1 in Week 1 instead of 0-1, getting rewarded for scoring a bunch of points.

No Kickers, Defenses, or Bonuses

All of them are too volatile. There's zero year-to-year correlation for kicker points, meaning they're just totally unpredictable. You could make an argument for team defenses deserving a spot, but not bonuses. Even though certain players are more likely than others to reach 100-yard and 300-yard milestones, deciding *which* of those elite options—players everyone owns—is a crapshoot.

Keeper vs. Dynasty

I'm a little bit torn on whether or not a keeper league or a true dynasty (retaining all players) is best. The reason is that, even though dynasty leagues require a deeper commitment and more research, they can unnecessarily punish you for one poor draft.

That's why (I think) I prefer a deep keeper league. In a league in which you can keep, say, seven players, you're strongly rewarded for quality drafting and forward-thinking, but not to such an extent that a great owner with a poor initial draft can't rebound.

I also prefer keeper leagues in which you lose a pick in the round in which your keepers were drafted. That basically gives each player a "contract," making keeper decisions more difficult and potentially opening up the pool of available players each year.

Auction Format

The biggest problem with fantasy football as it stands right now, in my opinion, is the unfairness of a traditional snake draft. There's just too much value at the top of the draft to make it fair. Even third-round reversal drafts, while superior to traditional 1-12, 12-1, 1-12 formats, create issues.

Auction drafts are naturally fairer than snake drafts. There are no draft slots to inhibit your ability to acquire players; if you want a guy, you can get him.

There's also way, way more strategy involved with auctions. You need to allocate cap space to each position, understanding market value and how the decisions of others affect your own. That's true (in a way) in traditional drafts, but not to the same degree.

And in keeper auction leagues, a player's "contract" is an actual dollar value. If you want to retain a player, you just give up the price at which you bought him (or the price plus X dollars) in the previous year.

And with that, I think I just fixed fantasy football.

7 How can I predict which running backs will break out?

"Running backs need to be quick, not necessarily fast. Quickness matters more than straight speed."

- Every NFL television analyst ever

In theory, it seems to make sense that running backs would benefit more from quickness than straight-line speed. They frequently work in traffic and certainly need the ability to make defenders miss in tight areas.

But I've shown in the past that straight-line speed, measured by the 40-yard dash, is highly predictive of NFL success for running backs. The running backs who post the best numbers continually run better than 4.50 in the 40-yard dash.

Yes, there are outliers. But for every Alfred Morris you can name, I can name five Ray Rice's (4.42, believe it or not).

In addition to speed, I want to see which other measurables might be predictive of NFL success for backs. So I charted some NFL Combine numbers for every running back drafted between 2008 and 2012. Then, I compared those numbers to each back's approximate value per year—an awesome judge of production on a per-season basis (so younger running backs aren't penalized for playing only a couple seasons).

The Correlations

Check out the strength of those relationships. Note that there's a negative correlation for every measurable except for the broad jump. That just means the longer a running

back's broad jump, the greater his NFL production.
Meanwhile, the lower the back's weight, 40 time, vertical,
short shuttle, three-come, and draft round, the better his
production.

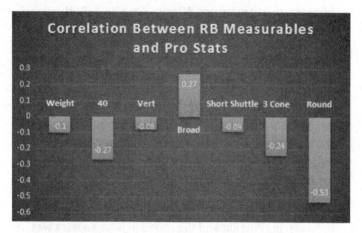

Let's take these one at a time.

Weight: There's a very weak relationship between weight
and pro stats, likely because lighter running backs can run
faster. Weight itself isn't inherently disadvantageous, it
seems, but it becomes a problem when it slows a running
back down. More to come on this.

40-Yard Dash: Not really a surprise here. The 40-yard dash
is the second-most predictive trait for running backs,
behind the round in which they were drafted.

Vertical: The negative correlation is surprising and
obviously just noise. If a lower vertical jump actually
helped players perform better, I'd be in the NFL. However,
I think the data definitely suggests something I've had a
hunch is true; the vertical jump doesn't matter. It doesn't
capture true explosiveness, which is what's important for
running backs.

Broad Jump: The broad jump is the most underrated physical test out there. Most NFL teams seem to care more about a player's vertical than his broad jump, but I've found that there's an extremely strong correlation between broad jump and 40-yard dash time. Both measure explosiveness in a way that the other tests can't.

Short Shuttle: There's no significant correlation between short shuttle time and running back success.

3 Cone: Surprisingly, the three-cone drill is much more strongly correlated with running back production than the short shuttle. I'm not sure I have an answer for this outside of the three-cone just being a better judge of explosiveness and change-of-direction.

Round: The strongest correlation of the bunch, by far, is between production and the round in which a back was drafted. This is all about highly drafted backs seeing the field more than mid and late-round picks (and it has almost nothing to do with actual talent).

Either way, a first-round running back selection will typically produce quality fantasy numbers just because he's going to see a heavy workload. The fact that he's not an outstanding player might not matter all that much in the short-term.

Weight and Speed

The moderate negative correlation between weight and NFL production for running backs was surprising, but I figured it's due to lighter running backs being faster and skewing the results.

So I charted every running back into one of 16 groups based on his speed and weight. Here's a heat map of the results, with darker being better.

	Sub-4.40	4.40-4.49	4.50-4.59	4.60+
Sub-200	4.26	6.07	3	NA
200 to 210	5.67	2.02	0.58	0.75
211 to 220	4.36	4.15	2.22	4.75
221+	1	4.71	1.69	2.5

You can see an obvious relationship between speed and running back success; almost all of the dark green boxes are near the left side, i.e. the speedsters.

However, there's not really too much of a relationship between weight and production, even after accounting for different subcategories of speed. That doesn't mean that extra weight is a bad thing (assuming the speed remains the same), but just that it really does appear to be less of a factor than what you might think.

If given the choice between a 220-pound back who runs a 4.45 and a 200-pound back who runs the same, I'm obviously taking the heavier player. But if we're talking about a 220-pound back in the 4.55 range, I'll take the lighter back all day long. Weight is great, but I have a need for speed.

Relationship Between 40-Yard Dash and Other Metrics
To better show why the numbers are the way they are, I want to take a quick look at the correlations between each measurable and the 40-yard dash. Remember, a player's numbers aren't independent of one another; weight

affects speed, explosive players will test well in a number of areas, and so on.

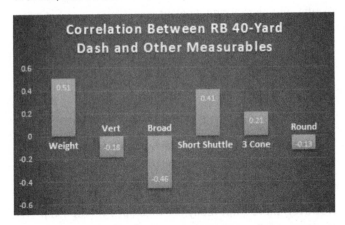

The strongest relationship here is unsurprisingly weight and speed; the heavier a running back, the slower he'll run. There's a mild correlation between the vertical jump and 40-yard dash, and the same goes for the three-cone drill.

Meanwhile, check out the strong relationship between the 40-yard dash and broad jump. Those backs who typically run really fast can also jump very far. The broad jump is more strongly correlated with the 40-yard dash than the short shuttle, which many might not initially assume to be true since the latter two are both tests of speed.

This is all pretty good evidence that we should be using the broad jump more in our assessment of running backs. It's perhaps just as good of an indicator of explosiveness as the 40-yard dash.

When a running back runs really fast but has a poor broad jump (Johnathan Franklin, for example), it might be a sign that he isn't quite as explosive as we think. If a back has only a decent 40-yard dash time but an outstanding broad jump (Michael Ford, for example), we might want to reconsider him as a potentially explosive running back.

Last, take a look at the relationship between the 40-yard dash and the round in which a running back is drafted; there's actually a negative correlation, meaning NFL teams have drafted slower running backs first!

You might take the strong correlation between draft round and production as evidence that teams are "getting it right" on running backs, but don't forget that the production is dependent on a heavy workload, which early-round backs obviously get.

In reality, running backs drafted in the late rounds have actually been more efficient than first and second-round backs on a per-carry basis! NFL teams are so bad at drafting running backs that you could completely randomize the order in which the backs get drafted and it wouldn't change much.

With the manner in which the 40 predicts running back success, it's absolutely shocking that NFL teams aren't valuing speed more in their assessment of running backs, and it stands as clear evidence that most NFL organizations still just don't get it.

8 Which measurables matter
for wide receivers?

They say that success equals opportunity plus preparation, but for NFL players, that simple equation needs to be refined. Namely, we need to add in "athleticism" as another variance.

Success = Opportunity + Preparation + Athleticism

That looks better. The reason that athleticism—which I'm using broadly here to encapsulate all physical measurables—is so important as a predictor is because we see the same types of players succeed again and again.

As I showed in the past, you want to search for explosive running backs, as measured by the 40-yard dash and broad jump, who were drafted highly. For tight ends, the draft round and vertical jump—a measurable that doesn't matter at all for running backs—are the best tools for forecasting success at the position.

Another reason that measurables are important is that they're often overlooked or misunderstood by fantasy owners. Prior to each season, we all have a pretty good idea of each player's projected workload. Opportunities are extremely important, but you aren't likely to obtain much of an advantage by out-projecting owners in that area.

Preparation is important, obviously, but I think it's a little bit overblown as a factor in predicting future success. For one, preparation should already be reflected in past statistics. If preparation really matters, it should show up on the field. And if it doesn't, well, who cares about it then? Second, we're dealing with professional athletes here. You might have the occasional lazy prospect, but for the most part, these guys are where they are because they've prepared for it.

Meanwhile, I rarely see fantasy owners looking up a potential draft pick's broad jump. But perhaps we should be doing that, especially with younger players.

The most obvious rebuttal is that NFL teams are relatively efficient at drafting, so the only thing that we really need to study when projecting young players is their draft round. Let the scouts do the work.

I don't really think NFL organizations are all that efficient at what they do, though. If they were, we wouldn't see players like Tavon Austin—who will continually be overvalued in standard fantasy leagues—or Robert Woods drafted ahead of guys like Keenan Allen. We wouldn't see Kendall Wright drafted higher than Alshon Jeffery. We certainly wouldn't see Joseph Randle ahead of both Andre Ellington and Zac Stacy (I made these claims prior to the respective players' careers, so it's not a 20/20 hindsight situation).

Draft round is important because it helps us predict opportunities, which are of course important. They're even more important for wide receivers than I previously thought.

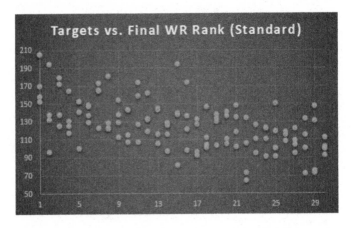

But again, short-term opportunities are easy for everyone to predict. If you can predict which types of players are worth their draft spot—and thus likely to *continue* to 1) receive opportunities to make plays well into the future and 2) actually make those plays—you'll be a step ahead of the competition.

Wide Receiver Measurables

I charted the Combine measurables for every wide receiver drafted over the past decade (excluding rookies from this year), comparing them to the players' approximate value (a metric that combines various stats like catches, yards, touchdowns, etc). Here's what I found.

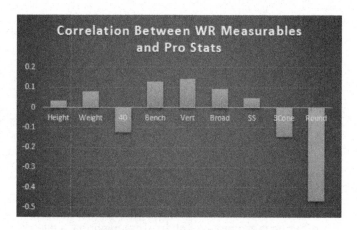

Note that it doesn't matter if the bars in the graph are positive or negative; all that matters is the length.

Again, draft round is the biggest predictor of future NFL success, and it isn't even close. But again, since pretty much everyone is going to be valuing that readily available information, you aren't going to be able to use it to acquire any sort of competitive advantage.

The next most predictive measurables for wide receivers, however, are ones that most of your competitors won't be examining—the three-cone drill and the vertical jump. We actually saw a very similar phenomenon with tight ends, which makes sense.

The vertical jump's worth to wide receivers and tight ends is pretty obvious, but what about the three-cone drill? I've found with every position that the three-cone drill (and the broad jump) are underrated explosiveness metrics. That's in opposition to the short shuttle, which is perhaps the most overrated measurable out there. The short shuttle isn't predictive for any position, but especially not for wide receivers; you can see the correlation between the short shuttle and wide receiver stats is positive, meaning wide receivers who have run slower in the short shuttle have actually been better in the NFL!

The most surprising data is that the correlation between height/weight and NFL success is relatively weak. That's really shocking to me since I've found that the best wide receivers are often big, strong players who can excel in the red zone in a consistent manner.

I think the numbers might be a little skewed by the fact that there are so many non-producing players in the data set. A lot of wide receivers get drafted, but few end up contributing meaningful numbers. That might have diluted the results just a bit.

Another possible explanation is that NFL teams aren't really valuing height and weight all that much, as we've seen with the recent early selections of players like Tavon Austin, Kendall Wright, and Randall Cobb. Those players are obviously given chances to succeed due to their draft slots, so their numbers are perhaps inflated from opportunities alone.

The reasons that I think both height and weight still matter quite a bit is that the game's *elite* wide receivers all have size in common. Take a look at the top 20 wide receivers in approximate value over the past decade.

	Height	Weight	40	Bench	Vert	Broad	Shuttle	3Cone	Round
Average	73	201.8	4.47	16	35.6	120.6	4.22	6.92	4
Top 20 Average	73.7	209.3	4.44	16.3	36.2	121.8	4.28	6.87	2.1

The elite class checks in better everywhere except for the short shuttle (surprise, surprise). But the gap in size, particularly weight, is largest. The top 20 wide receivers over the last 10 seasons have weighed over 209 pounds. The average drafted wide receiver who attended the NFL Scouting combine weighed just 201.8 pounds. Compare that to only moderate jumps in the 40-yard dash, bench, vertical, broad jump, and three-cone drill.

Because of that, my conclusion is that different types of wide receivers can be productive, namely those who are drafted highly. But the dominant wide receivers—the Calvin Johnson, Dez Bryant, Demaryius Thomas, Julio Jones, A.J. Green, Brandon Marshall, Alshon Jeffery, Josh Gordon, Andre Johnson, Vincent Jackson-esque players— might not all run that fast or have elite broad jumps, but they all possess elite size.

9 Is there one number that predicts tight end success?

Tight end is a weird position. Whereas I believe there are factors that heavily influence fantasy production at the quarterback, running back, and wide receiver positions, I'm not sure that's the case at tight end. It's the most difficult position to project, in my view—even more so than wide receiver.

At quarterback, I care primarily about workload and percentage of touchdowns. I want passers who will throw the ball often and account for a high rate of their team's touchdowns. Mobility is also important. At running back, I concern myself with workload and straight-line speed. At wide receiver, I don't care so much about 40 times, instead looking at size and red zone efficiency. I want big receivers who will score.

Tight end is most like wide receiver, but the size seems to be less important because they're all big. Whereas wide receivers like Brandon Marshall are far better red zone options than smaller options like Percy Harvin, pretty much every tight end is large enough to be red zone efficient.

Further, NFL teams use tight ends in different ways. That's immediately evident when you consider there are two tight ends who are so far ahead of the pack that they completely alter the way fantasy owners need to approach the position.

So to see if there are any factors that heavily influence tight end production, I analyzed every player at the position who attended the NFL Scouting Combine and was drafted in the past decade. I compared their approximate value with measurables from NFLCombineResults.com.

Here are the correlations...

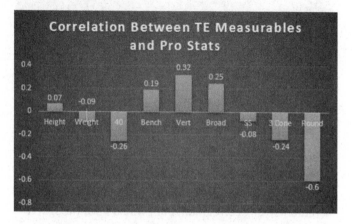

It doesn't matter if a coefficient is positive or negative; all that matters is the length. And you can see with a strength of correlation of 0.60, the biggest predictor of tight end fantasy success, by far, is draft round. That's not really surprising since highly drafted tight ends get the most opportunities to make plays.

Before analyzing this in more detail, check out the running back graph as a means of comparison...

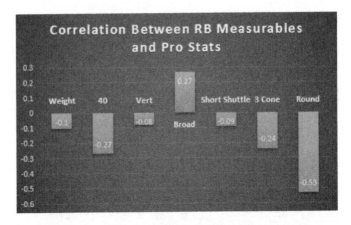

The tight end graph has height and bench press as extra factors. While height has been mildly predictive of success, the bench press results (0.19) are surprising. That's not an incredibly strong correlation, but I would have thought it would be basically zero.

Otherwise, it's incredible how similarly the measurables predict success for both running backs and tight ends. Here's the difference in the coefficients for each measurable:

Weight: 0.01

40-Yard Dash: 0.01

Vertical: 0.40

Broad Jump: 0.02

Short Shuttle: 0.01

Three-Cone Drill: 0.00

Draft Round: 0.07

Unbelievable. Pretty much every measurable is indistinguishable except draft round (to a small degree) and the vertical jump (to an incredible extent). The draft round is understandable since running back is probably the most dependent position on the field, to the point that late-round rookies can make immediate impacts.

But the difference in the importance of the vertical for tight ends and running backs is stunning. It's pretty clear evidence that vertical explosiveness, while not at all important for running backs, is extremely valuable to tight ends who frequently need to attack the football and come down with it in traffic.

The numbers are also a great example of where non-stat geeks can go wrong when analyzing numbers. Everyone uses numbers to prove their points, even if it's something as simple as touchdowns or yards. But the analytics-minded paradoxically tend to limit the quantity of stats they're willing to analyze.

In the case of running backs, the vertical jump is clearly not important. It's not important because it's not predictive. That's not the case for tight ends, displaying why some stats need to be taken with a grain of salt. We can't just use a single stat as the be-all end-all for each position. The 40-yard dash matters a lot for some positions, but not at all for others. We can look at all the numbers in the world, but the only ones that truly count are the ones that help us make better predictions.

For tight ends, that's draft slot and the vertical jump.

10 Which measurable is the most overrated?

One of the misconceptions about stat heads or anyone who places heavy emphasis on data in football/fantasy football is that we care about all numbers the same.

The truth is that most people who use analytics in fantasy football reject *most* stats, labeling them as explanatory rather than predictive, i.e. for prediction purposes, they're worthless. In many ways, stat geeks are just more discriminating in regards to which numbers they'll use; they use *fewer* stats than the general public, just better ones.

For example, prior to the 2013 NFL Draft, I mentioned that wide receiver Keenan Allen moved up my board quite a bit. I got a few responses to the tune of "But Allen's 40 suks n thats all u care about. Your a f'ing moran."

I might be a "moran," but the stats I care about most are those that are going to help me make better predictions and win fantasy football leagues. More speed is better for every position, but it's not all that vital for wide receivers, who thrive on size. So us stat geeks aren't just sitting around and jacking each other off every time someone runs a 4.3. I care a whole lot about straight-line speed for running backs, but for the majority of positions, the 40-yard dash isn't terribly important.

Predictive of Success

Measurables are important for fantasy owners because it's really easy to create models, form hypotheses, and most important, test our theories to improve our approach to the game. I'd argue a stat geek can give you more insights (and accuracy) into a particular draft class in a few hours with a spreadsheet than all of the cumulative hours put in by some team's scouts over the course of a year. If that weren't true, we probably wouldn't see Trent Richardson drafted in the top five, Tavon Austin in the top 10, or Mark Ingram in the first round.

The most important thing we need from a measurable is that it can help us make better predictions regarding a player's future. One of the common qualms with the 40-yard dash is that "players almost never run 40 yards in a straight line during games."

To which I respond: Whooooo carrrrrrrreeeeessss?

Employers don't ask current workers to take IQ tests as part of the job, but they sure can help predict who's best for it. The 40-yard dash and other measurables are like IQ tests; the performance is representative of something that might or might not help an employer. For certain positions, a particular measurable might not matter as much as for other positions, much like an IQ test is probably a better predictor of success for a chemist than a cashier.

The Most Overrated and Underrated Measurables

By looking at a particular measurable and stacking it up against NFL production, we can test how strongly the two have been correlated in the past. In doing that, it's clear that the short shuttle is one of the most overrated measurables out there.

I charted the strength of the correlation between the short shuttle and NFL production (in terms of approximate value) for the running back, wide receiver, and tight end positions. To give you an idea of the weakness of the relationship, I charted it next to the broad jump, which I believe is one of the most underrated metrics.

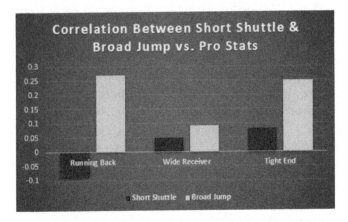

For the short shuttle, a negative correlation means that as the time goes down (meaning it gets better), NFL production increases. Shockingly, the short shuttle correlation is negative only for running backs, meaning that as times for wide receivers and tight ends have increased (gotten worse), NFL production has actually improved! That suggests the short shuttle has no predictive ability for pass-catchers.

Further, the strength of the correlation between short shuttle times and running back success is just (-.09), which is almost nothing. How many times have you heard a TV analyst say that a running back needs to be "quicker than fast?" I think Mike Mayock even has a "QTF" tattoo on his lower back. Unfortunately, running backs don't need to be "quicker than fast." They need explosiveness, represented in both straight-line speed and the broad jump.

Like the 40-yard dash, the broad jump is a maneuver that you'll never see an NFL player complete on the field during a game. As much as I'd like to see Eli Manning forced to broad jump for the win, it's not happening.

And again, whooooooooo carrrrreeeeessss? The broad jump is very representative of explosiveness. Because of that, there's a strong correlation between a player's broad jump and 40-yard dash. Both metrics are most important at positions that require the greatest degree of explosiveness. For so long, we thought wide receivers needed explosiveness more than just about any other position. It's far more important for running backs, though, as evidenced by the graph.

Fantasy Implications

As I've mentioned, measurables have less and less impact on player projections as the players gain more NFL experience. I care a whole lot about a running back's 40-yard dash when he's a rookie, a little less after he has a season's worth of NFL touches, a little less still after two seasons, and so on.

Still, there are so few NFL games in a season and players are so dependent on one another for success that we can really use measurables to project performance even after a player has been in the league a handful of years.

For example, assume you're trying to predict the play of a 25-year old running back who was really successful in one city but signed as a free agent elsewhere. Since running back play is so dependent on the offensive line, it's not out of the question for a back to see sustained success in spite of lackluster talent. If his offensive line situation changes and you need to assess his true skill level, the 40-yard dash and broad jump can help do that.

Measurables are important, but we need to understand how to best utilize them; different metrics are valuable for different positions, just as is the case with other jobs. The 40-yard dash, broad jump, vertical, and so on can all help us more accurately forecast NFL player performance for different positions.

Regardless of the position, though, it appears as though the short shuttle is not very representative of future NFL play. Even if there is a relationship there, it would be difficult to acquire value by emphasizing it since the majority of NFL teams factor it into their rankings to a degree that's stronger than the measurable's actual worth. And since your fantasy draft will be a reflection of the NFL draft when it comes to rookies, that means that you, too, won't find value by emphasizing the short shuttle and, perhaps, could even acquire value by intentionally seeking players who performed poorly in the drill but showed explosiveness elsewhere.

11 How many fantasy points can I expect from different types of rookies?

Despite the fact that the majority of NFL organizations seem to make draft picks using a combination of a Ouija board and, even worse, the opinion of scouts, the top draft picks still turn into the best pros. That's probably mainly a self-fulfilling prophecy since the highest picks get the most playing time and far more opportunities to show they can produce.

It doesn't really matter *why* the highest draft choices record the best fantasy numbers; for our purposes, we just want to know how much better a first-rounder is than, say, a third-round pick, and how we can use that data to predict rookie stats at each position.

Here's how rookies in each draft round have been able to contribute since 2000.

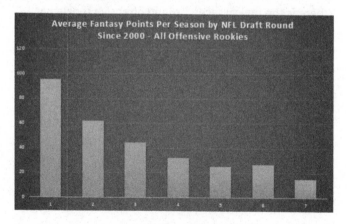

Third-round picks have provided around half as much bulk production as first-rounders. Interestingly, the difference between a fourth and sixth-rounder hasn't been all that much. Once you get into the back half of the draft, the difference in the quality of prospects is minimal.

As we'd expect, there are obvious differences in production for different positions. Take a look at quarterbacks.

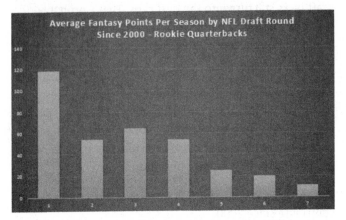

Whereas the typical second-round offensive rookie has produced around two-thirds as many fantasy points as the typical first-rounder, the average second-round quarterback checks in at well below half of the number of points from a first-round quarterback. Second-rounders have actually been worse than both third and fourth-round quarterbacks, so once you get out of the first round (and really, the top half of the first round), the chances for rookie fantasy production at the quarterback position are slim.

The running back position has a flatter distribution.

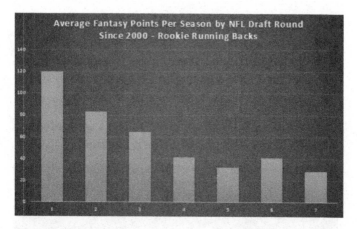

Both second and third-round running backs have produced well over half of the production of first-rounders. Late-round running backs have lagged behind, but there have still been plenty of usable rookies at the position who were drafted late (think Alfred Morris and Zac Stacy).

The running back graph actually shows just how much usage affects production. If you recall from some of my other work, I've found that mid and late-round running backs have actually been *more* efficient on a per-carry basis than first and second-rounders.

But since teams give their early picks more playing time, they score way more fantasy points. Running backs are so dependent on a heavy workload for production that the graph appears to show that first-round running backs are much better players than mid and late-rounders when, in reality, they're just given more touches.

If you're choosing between rookie runners who are comparable in every way except their draft slot, you're better off going with the one drafted higher—not because he's better, but because his team *thinks* he's better. That changes if you have good evidence that a mid or late-rounder will receive a hefty workload, however. If you know a talented fifth-round rookie is going to be his team's starter, you can let fellow owners jump all over the higher-drafted rookies so that you can pick up comparable fantasy production at a much cheaper price.

The wide receiver position has had almost a completely linear fantasy distribution based on draft round.

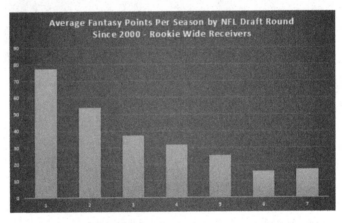

Although rookie wide receivers are poor values without elite upside as a whole, that changes if you implement stricter requirements as to which players you'll select—namely, big receivers who dominated in college and get selected in the top six or so selections.

And finally, let's take a look at the tight ends.

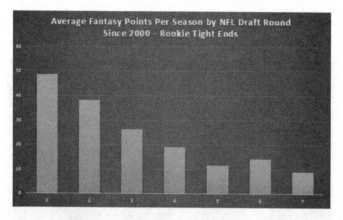

The biggest difference between the tight ends and other positions is that there's not too big of a drop from the first round to the second. That makes sense, since the majority of first-round tight ends have been selected in the bottom half of the round. There are very few Vernon Davis-esque tight ends out there, so you're more likely to see second-round tight ends resemble first-rounders than you are at any other position.

Comparing Positions

The rates of decline by draft round are important in understanding how different types of rookies at different positions can help you. But certain positions of course translate better from college to the NFL, allowing for usable fantasy contributions right out of the gate.

Using the data from the positional graphs, I charted the average fantasy points for first and second-rounders at all positions. In normal redraft leagues, it's these players you will normally target. You might also consider mid and late-round rookie running backs in particular situations, but the majority of the top fantasy producers even at the running back position will be those drafted early.

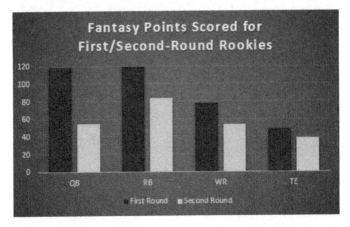

It's really telling that rookie running backs have out-produced quarterbacks, even though quarterbacks as a whole normally score more fantasy points than running backs. When you view production in this manner, you can also see how much more valuable rookie running backs are than both wide receivers and tight ends. Historically, second-round running backs have tallied more points than first-round wide receivers.

These numbers support the notion that rookie runners are undervalued, while rookie pass-catchers usually get over-drafted. If there's one rule I could create for drafting rookies at each position in redraft leagues, here they are: 1) draft only first-round quarterbacks who are mobile, 2) load up on rookie running backs who can catch passes, especially late in your fantasy draft, 3) avoid rookie receivers, except the truly elite options, and 4) if you draft a rookie tight end, fade the first-rounders, who will go higher in your fantasy draft, in favor of a second-rounder who probably has the same level of talent.

12 How much does a heavy workload Matter to running backs?

Heading into his Week 8 matchup with the Seattle Seahawks, no one seemed particularly high on St. Louis Rams running Zac Stacy. The fifth-round rookie out of Vanderbilt had taken his first 50 NFL carries for 214 yards—a rather pedestrian 4.28 YPC.

There were other reasons to like Stacy, though. I did a pre-draft scouting report on the running back in which I said this:

> *On film, it's hard not to draw a comparison between Stacy and Ray Rice, although Rice is a faster player. The best comparison might very well be this one:*
>
> ***Zac Stacy***: *5-9, 216 pounds, 3,143 yards, 5.4 YPC, 4.55 40-yard dash, 6.70 three-cone drill, 4.17 short shuttle, 27 reps*
>
> ***Player X***: *5-9, 215 pounds, 3,431 yards, 5.6 YPC, 4.55 40-yard dash, 6.79 three-cone drill, 4.16 short shuttle, 28 reps*
>
> *So who is Player X? Another late-round running back? Nope, it's 2012 first-rounder Doug Martin— the same Doug Martin who rushed for 1,454 yards and caught 49 passes as a rookie.*

Martin doesn't look so hot right now, but the point is that Stacy possesses the requisite physical tools to succeed in the NFL. He's not blazing fast, but he's fast enough, given his weight, to be productive.

But here's the real reason that we should have foreseen Stacy's Week 8 breakout for 134 yards and Week 9 outburst for 127 yards and two scores: he started to get more carries.

I've often talked about the importance of a heavy workload for running backs. As much as I seek running backs with speed, the majority of running back fantasy points come courtesy of a heavy workload.

If you think about it, that makes sense. The deviation in running back efficiency is pretty small, with below-average backs checking in under 4.0 YPC and the NFL's leaders usually hovering in the 5.5 YPC range.

Meanwhile, the difference in carries for two starting running backs can be substantial. In 2012, for example, Adrian Peterson led the league in rushes with 351. There were only 23 other backs in the whole league who had even half that many carries. Only six backs had 80 percent as many carries as Peterson.

So we know that a heavy workload is important—more important than talent, in fact, outside of talent being a factor in playing time (which isn't really a huge deal since NFL teams are horribly inefficient at understanding which running backs are the most valuable).

But how much? How much do carries matter compared to YPC when it comes to a running backs' fantasy status?

I compiled the carries and YPC for the top 120 backs from the past four seasons to examine the correlation between the two stats and a running back's year-end rank.

Here are the running backs charted in terms of YPC:

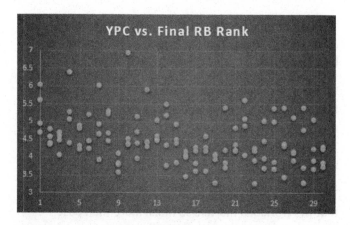

It turns out that the coefficient of determination for YPC and running back fantasy rank is -0.33. That means that there's a moderately strong relationship between YPC and fantasy points; as YPC goes up, final rank improves. But as you can see by the scattered nature of the dots in the plot, the relationship isn't overwhelmingly strong.

Let's take a look at carries versus final rank:

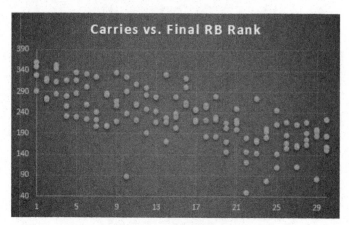

Here, you can see a much stronger relationship. Outside of a handful of outliers (I'm looking at you Darren Sproles), all of the running backs fall within a pretty narrow range. The strength of this correlation is -.71. That's more than twice as strong as the relationship between YPC and running back success.

Whether you play season-long leagues and you're looking for a spot start or daily leagues and you need a cheap running back option, the key is to search for players like Tampa Bay's Mike James who are going to see big workloads.

That might seem intuitive, but it's probably not as obvious that the workload matters so much more than past efficiency that, on a week-to-week basis, you can almost ignore talent solely in favor of opportunity.

13 How much does a heavy workload affect wide receiver production?

One of my favorite aspects of playing and writing about fantasy football is disproving conventional wisdom. I've done that with "truisms" such as running backs break down after X touches and rookie wide receivers make for high-upside selections.

When I'm brainstorming ideas for articles, I tend to think about arguments that I believe to be true, but for which I don't actually have any data, then research them to see if they hold water. I did that recently with the idea that running backs need lots of carries to produce, which turned out to indeed be true.

Well, I've often wondered how much targets affect wide receivers. It's obvious that more targets is better, but to what degree? My initial hunch was that since there can be huge deviations in yards per reception for pass-catchers, the number of targets wouldn't matter nearly as much as the number of carries for running backs.

After running the numbers, it turns out that while targets aren't quite as vital as carries, a receiver's workload is much more crucial to his production than I previously thought—way more valuable than his efficiency.

Before getting into the data, consider this stat. In 2012, there were only four receivers in the NFL who finished outside of the top 35 in targets but inside the top 30 in fantasy rank. That means that 26 of the top 30 wide receivers in fantasy were also ranked in the top 35 in targets, which is pretty incredible. Those four receivers were T.Y. Hilton and THREE players from Green Bay—Jordy Nelson, James Jones, and Randall Cobb.

So a basic rule-of-thumb for wide receivers is that unless they play with Aaron Rodgers, there's almost zero chance of them finishing in the top 30 at the position with fewer than 90 targets. And to have a legitimate shot, it should really be closer to 100 or even 110.

The Numbers

So with that said, let's take a look at the correlation between a few stats and final wide receiver fantasy rank over the past four seasons. Note that all the correlations are negative because as each increase, final wide receiver rank decreases (meaning it improves).

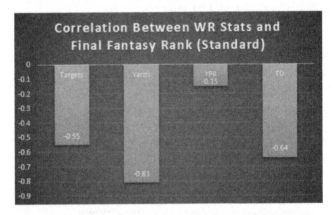

It's a little surprising to me that the wide receivers who've put up the most yards have been more valuable than those with the most touchdowns. Yards account for a greater percentage of points, but there's more deviation in touchdowns. I've actually built my wide receiver corps around red zone ability in recent years—which I'll likely continue to do since it's such a consistent stat from year to year—but the receivers with the most points are more likely to lead the league in yards than touchdowns.

It's not at all shocking that yards and touchdowns are the most strongly correlated with fantasy rank since they're a component of it; fantasy owners get points for yards and scores, not for targets or YPR. But take a look at the difference between those latter two stats: a -0.55 correlation coefficient for targets, compared to just -0.15 for YPR.

Although there's still a correlation between YPR and wide receiver rank, it's rather insignificant compared to that for targets. If you want to project touchdowns and especially yards, you're better off doing your best to accurately predict targets instead of YPR.

To see that difference visualized, I plotted the top 30 receivers from each of the past four seasons in terms of YPR and fantasy rank.

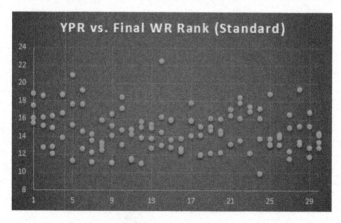

There's basically no trend here at all. On the other hand, take a look at targets vs. fantasy rank.

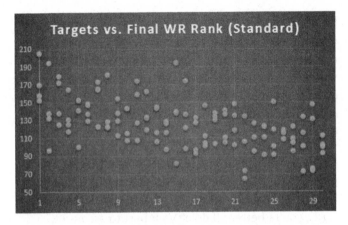

Clearly a more linear relationship. Of the wide receivers to finish in the top five over the past four seasons, only Jordy Nelson in 2011 had fewer than 100 targets (and he scored 15 times). Meanwhile, no wide receiver to finish first has had fewer than 153 targets, with the average being 171.5.

It appears as though a wide receiver's workload is way more vital to his production than I initially believed. And if you're going to bank on a team's No. 2 wide receiver who you know won't have a realistic shot at more than 110 or so targets, he better be one heck of a red zone threat.

14 Do running backs really break down after high-volume seasons?
Data collected by Ian Hartitz

In 1998, Atlanta Falcons running back Jamaal Anderson tore up the league with 1,846 rushing yards and 16 total touchdowns while carrying the ball an NFL-record 410 times. That's nearly 26 attempts per game.

The massive workload appeared to take a toll on Anderson; he played in only two games the following season and averaged just 3.6 YPC during the rest of his NFL career—a career that lasted only 21 more games.

Anderson's case is extreme, but not totally unusual; anecdotally, there seems to be a whole lot of evidence that running backs coming off of high-volume seasons tend to break down in some way the next year. If you ask the average fantasy football player if running backs break down after receiving lots of carries, he's going to respond "of course" and cite Anderson or some other back who garnered lots of touches and was never the same.

I broke down this concept in my first book, but I wanted to come back to it to 1) update the past data, 2) provide new data, and 3) propose some unique thoughts on the subject. So do running backs really suffer after high-volume seasons? Let's take a look.

The Data on Running Backs Breaking Down
Let me save you the suspense: the numbers are overwhelmingly in support of high-volume running backs regressing in the year following a heavy workload. Take a look at how 300-carry running backs from 2003 to 2013—

of which there were 75—fared in the following year (Year X+1).

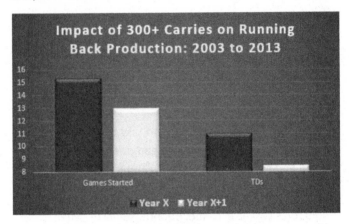

Massive drops—a 15 percent decline in games started and a 23 percent decline in touchdowns. That's pretty startling and of obvious concern for fantasy owners. Running backs coming off of seasons with 300-plus carries have scored exactly 2.5 fewer touchdowns in the following year, on average, which is 15 fantasy points—or about one fantasy point per game from touchdowns alone.

There are other declines in production, too. Take a look at the average number of attempts and rushing yards.

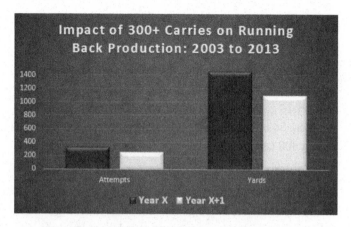

The typical 300-carry running back has seen a massive 22 percent decline in rushing attempts and an even bigger 25 percent drop in rushing yards. If you picked a 300-carry back out of a hat and were asked to predict his rushing yards in Year X+1, you'd probably have a pretty accurate projection if you just sliced his rushing yards by one-quarter.

Well, these numbers are pretty conclusive, right? Not so fast my friend...

Why the Numbers Are Misleading

When we're analyzing any sample of players, we need to ask ourselves if they're representative of the conclusions we draw and if there's any sort of selection bias at work. A selection bias is an error in choosing individuals in a study.

While there's not necessarily an "error" in analyzing 300-carry running backs to see if they become overworked, there's still a bias toward the type of running backs who reach that threshold of work. Namely, a running back needs certain things to go right for him to see such a heavy workload.

First, he needs to be healthy. Running backs get injured all the time, and I'd argue that no running back is ever likely to start 16 games in a season. That's just the nature of the position. So unusual health is basically a prerequisite for seeing 300 carries.

Second, they need to be efficient. A running back who is averaging 3.5 YPC after 10 games probably won't see a whole lot of carries moving forward. Thus, most high-volume running backs are rushing at a decent level of efficiency.

So what we're really looking at when we examine high-volume running backs is a group that's benefited from better-than-average health and better-than-average efficiency. Both of those things are influenced heavily by randomness, and thus likely to regress in the future. A running back who starts all 16 games is probably going to start fewer games in the following season whether he had a lot of carries or not. Similarly, a running back who rushes for 5.0 YPC is very likely to check in below that number in the next year, again regardless of his workload.

In effect, what we're saying is "running backs who are unusually healthy and probably have higher-than-normal efficiency will have worse health and efficiency the following season." That's pretty obvious though, right?

Here's how running back efficiency has tanked after a season with 300-plus carries.

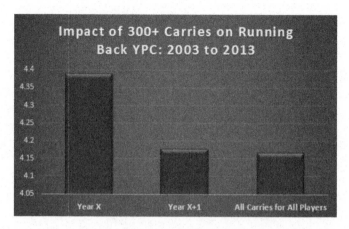

Running backs who have rushed 300 or more times over the past decade have averaged 4.39 YPC during their high-volume season and just 4.18 YPC the next year—a small but meaningful drop of 4.8 percent.

But here's the key: take a look at the rushing efficiency for all players on all carries during that time. At 4.17 YPC, it's actually worse than the 300-carry backs in Year X+1. That suggests that backs aren't falling off of a cliff after seasons with high volume, but rather just regressing naturally. Since the sample of 300-carry backs is naturally skewed to include mainly just those backs with high efficiency, we'd expect a drop in YPC whether they get "overworked" or not.

To lend more credence to that idea, I charted the efficiency of high-volume running backs as the season progresses. If lots of carries really take a toll on a running back, we'd expect decreased efficiency late in the year.

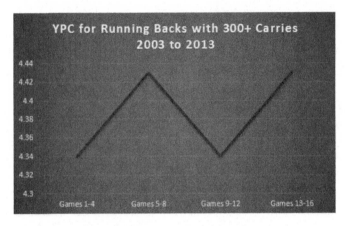

There's no trend here at all. In the final four games of the season, running backs with 300 or more carries have actually been at their best, averaging 4.43 YPC. They don't seem to be breaking down at all. What we're seeing is normal regression toward the mean that's creating the illusion of wear and tear.

The Effect of Age

Very quickly, I want to touch on another potential issue—that running backs as a whole are normally going to be less efficient than they were the previous season.

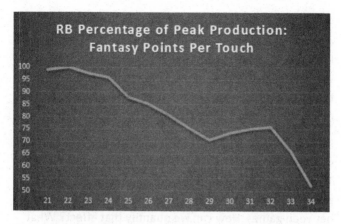

The average age for running backs with 300-plus carries during the time I studied was 26.3-years-old. That's right in the midst of a very steep yearly decline for the position as a whole, meaning at least part of the drop in efficiency that we see is due to the aging process.

Summing It Up

Do running backs really get overworked? I don't think so, and if there is an effect, it's likely so small that we can't turn it into actionable information. We do see a steep regression in health, efficiency, and bulk stats in running backs who garner lots of carries in a given year, but that's due almost entirely to the nature of that sample of runners—unusually healthy and efficient, and thus in position to post quality bulk stats.

If we analyze all running backs who have abnormal health or very high efficiency in a given season, we see that they also regress in the following year; it likely has very little to do with workload. It's just regression toward the mean.

Further, if you really think about the idea that a few extra carries are going to wear down a running back, it's silly. First, why use 300 carries (or 280, or any other number)? We have to pick a "line in the sand" to study, but it's totally arbitrary. Is a 300-carry back really going to be much worse than a 280-carry running back?

Second, running backs get touches other ways. These studies frequently don't include receptions, but why not? They also don't include practice reps. Teams hit in practice, and some coaches work their players rather hard between games. How can we quantify that effect? What about runners who don't take a lot of big hits (such as a guy like LeSean McCoy) versus players who get hit hard on nearly every run (like Adrian Peterson)?

If there's a reason to be scared off by a high-volume back, it would be his age. But that really has nothing to do with the carries and everything to do with running backs naturally breaking down as they get older.

So should you avoid high-volume backs? After all, they do see a steep decline in production in Year X+1. The answer is no, not at all. They're unlikely to repeat their big season, but that's due to that year being an outlier. If you're betting on a running back to remain healthy and record above-average efficiency, there's probably a slightly better chance that a high-volume back will do it than one with moderate "tread on the tires."

In a day and age when there are only a handful of workhorse running backs remaining in the league, there's simply no reason to bypass one because he's coming off a season with some arbitrarily high number of carries; he's likely to regress, but his chances of matching Year X's production in Year X+1 are probably about the same as they were prior to Year X.

Heavily worked running backs will normally see a drop in health and efficiency in the future, but those declines are only correlated with a heavy workload and not caused by it. When it comes to actionable intel, there's not much to be gleaned from a running back's previous workload.

15 Should I pair a quarterback with his receiver(s)?

Data contributed by Ian Hartitz

Since I jumped into the world of daily fantasy football, I've developed a new way to look at the week-to-week grind in season-long formats. That resulted primarily from working with DraftKings on my last daily fantasy sports book, as they supplied me with a whole bunch of incredible data that altered the way I approach weekly fantasy football decisions.

One of the most popular tactics in daily fantasy football is known as "stacking." Technically speaking, stacking is using a whole bunch of players from the same team—most popular in baseball—but the term has been loosened to include quarterback/wide receiver pairings.

Naturally, we kind of know that pairing a wide receiver with his quarterback is going to increase upside and risk at the same time since the duo is dependent on one another for production. If you look at the numbers, you see a ridiculously strong relationship between quarterback and wide receiver fantasy points. From *Fantasy Football (and Baseball) for Smart People*:

> *When playing daily fantasy football, you can increase upside by pairing your quarterback with one of his receivers. If the quarterback has a big day, which is pretty much a prerequisite for taking down a tourney, it's highly likely that your pass-catcher will produce as well. Take a look at the strong correlation between quarterback points and team wide receiver points.*

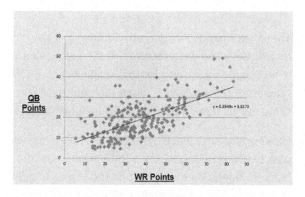

When a quarterback has at least 30 points on DraftKings, there's roughly a 91.7 percent chance that his wide receivers will combine for 30 or more points, an 83.3 percent chance of them checking in above 40 points, a two-in-three probability of 50-plus points, and incredibly a one-in-three chance of at least 70 combined points.

That last tidbit is really surprising—a one-in-three chance of 70 combined receiver points when a quarterback posts 30? That's ridiculous.

So to say stacking in daily fantasy football tournaments is a smart strategy is an understatement; pretty much every top player pairs a quarterback with at least one of his wide receivers in every large league.

In season-long formats, though, you're not concerned solely with upside, but also consistency on a week-to-week basis. We know that stacking is volatile, but can the upside make up for the inconsistency? Let's find out.

The Relationship Between QB and WR Production

There are a handful of ways to determine if pairing a quarterback and wide receiver on the same team is "worth it" in traditional fantasy football leagues. I chose to look at how often receivers kill it when their quarterbacks do the same versus how frequently the two "tank" together.

Looking at quarterbacks who played full seasons over the past two years, I broke down their production into buckets, analyzing their top four and top eight games. Here's how the production for their WR1 and WR2 looks in those buckets.

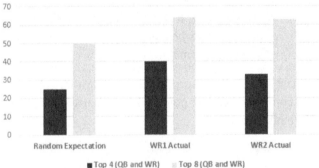

If a wide receiver's play weren't tied to that of his quarterback, we'd expect a wide receiver to have a top four fantasy game—that is, one of his best four games on the year—25 percent of the time when his quarterback does the same. So we're looking at a quarterback's top four (or top eight) fantasy games, then determining how frequently his wide receivers turn in the same sort of performance.

Well, both WR1s and WR2s produce top four and top eight games at a rate greater than what would be produced from chance alone, which is what we'd expect. When a quarterback has a top four performance, there's a 40 percent chance that his No. 1 wide receiver also has a top four performance and a 33 percent chance that it happens for his No. 2 wide receiver.

Not surprisingly, WR1 production is more closely linked to his quarterback than WR2 production. That means that pairing a top receiver with his quarterback possesses more upside than doing the same with a No. 2 receiver and his quarterback. But is it much riskier, too?

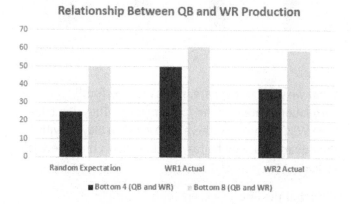

Relationship Between QB and WR Production

Here, I'm looking at the same thing as the first graph, except with bottom four/eight performances. So a quarterback lays a dud (one of his worst four/eight games); how likely is it that his wide receivers did the same?

Again, the results exceed the random expectations. But there's actually a stronger correlation than with the top performances; WR1s have a 50 percent chance of having one of their worst four performances of the year when their quarterback does the same. The rate is 38 percent for WR2s.

Now let's compare that risk with the upside from graph one.

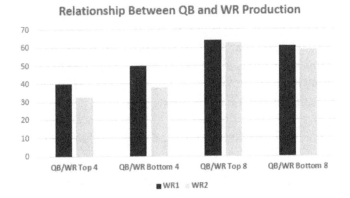

Relationship Between QB and WR Production

What we want to see here is that the "top four" correlations outweigh the "bottom four." They don't. For both WR1s and WR2s, there's more risk in playing with their quarterback on fantasy football teams than there is upside.

Note that the effect switches with "top eight" performances, but just slightly. Those results aren't significant, while the gap in the "top four" category is meaningful.

When to Stack

One of the important things to remember in head-to-head season-long leagues is that consistency can matter as much as total points. We always want players projected to score a shitload of points, but it's preferable to create a team that has a high floor from week to week.

Stacking a wide receiver with his quarterback decreases your floor, and it doesn't seem that your team's week-to-week ceiling will rise enough to compensate for the downside. You're kind of creating an asymmetrical team—which is actually the goal—but in the wrong direction.

So should you ever stack? You should do it all the time if you need upside when playing daily fantasy football. Even in season-long formats, I wouldn't avoid pairing a quarterback with his wide receiver at all costs.

When a wide receiver is almost the sole focus of his quarterback—like the Stafford-to-Johnson connection in Detroit—it creates a more volatile relationship. Compare that to a pair like Jay Cutler and Alshon Jeffery; Jeffery has Brandon Marshall opposite him to draw coverage and, although a great performance from Cutler obviously helps Jeffery, he's not as dependent on Cutler as Marshall since he's a WR2.

It really comes down to targets. When a wide receiver sees a lot of targets—as in a WR1—he's less likely to "get lucky" in regards to efficiency. As sample size increases, numbers regress toward the mean. Compare that to a WR2 who sees fewer overall targets, and thus a more volatile distribution from week to week. He's more likely to be able to turn in one of his better games, even if his quarterback isn't on point, because he doesn't need a truly elite game (like a WR1) to have a top four performance.

Weighing the Cost

Another huge factor at play is the cost. Spending a second and third-round pick on a wide receiver and quarterback who play on the same team is expensive and risky. You don't want to bypass teammates if both are of obvious value, but when things are close, it's best to diversify in a head-to-head format. That could change in a total-points league, by the way, since you don't need consistency on a weekly basis.

When the cost is lower, though, pairing teammates can be an incredibly shrewd strategy. Let's say you have your starters set and you're entering the 12th round looking for a backup quarterback. In this situation, I almost always try to pair one with one of his wide receivers already on my roster, assuming the value is close.

To me, there's immense value in pairing one of your top wide receivers with his quarterback as the backup on your fantasy team. You acquire the potential upside of that combination, but you don't need to start the duo together during most weeks since you have a better signal-caller on the roster, thus limiting the risk.

There are two main advantages to his strategy. The first is that you can potentially play the duo together if you run into a dominant opponent. Let's say it's Week 12 and you're on the playoff bubble. You're facing the top team in your league, so you want as much upside as possible to take down his powerhouse. As FDR might say, with great upside comes great stackability. Pair your wide receiver with his backup quarterback to increase your team's ceiling.

The second advantage—the bigger one—is that pairing your backup quarterback with one of his wide receivers creates built-in upside in your lineup in the event of an injury. If you were to lose your top quarterback, your team would immediately become an underdog in a lot of situations. Again, you need upside, which is automatically created when your backup quarterback moves into the starting role; you have a natural stack in place every week, giving you the upside to overcome the injury.

So in short, it's probably best to avoid high-priced stacks, but stacking teammates when at least one has a low price tag is not only acceptable, but preferred.

Note: In the middle of this lesson, I used the term "lays a dud." Well, I originally typed "lays a dude" by accident and missed it after editing the article. For some reason, I decided to go over it again. I was one fluke decision away from publishing "So a quarterback lays a dude." That would have changed the direction of this lesson in a hurry.

16 How can I see explosive growth in fantasy point scoring?

If you told me 10 years ago that I'd write a title with the phrase "explosive growth in fantasy," I probably. . .would have believed you, to be honest.

Exponential growth, which we all know is just so hot right now, isn't really sought in fantasy football because, in most cases, fantasy points are accumulated in a linear way. Below, the line that has no curve represents linear growth, while the line that starts slowly and ultimately ends up on top represents exponential growth.

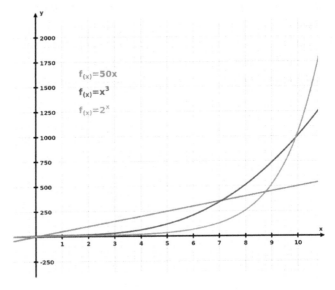

If you have a retirement plan, you're hoping to maintain it long enough that you can continue to see exponential growth through compounded interest. In such a situation, your interest grows very slowly at first and very rapidly as your plan matures. Here's a very cool visualization of exponential growth.

So can we generate a snowball effect in fantasy football? I think there are a few situations that either represent exponential growth or are at least similar in nature.

Red Zone Studs

The most obvious example of exponential growth in fantasy points comes with touchdowns. As offenses approach the goal line, their probability of scoring a touchdown increases in a non-linear way. Per Advanced NFL Stats:

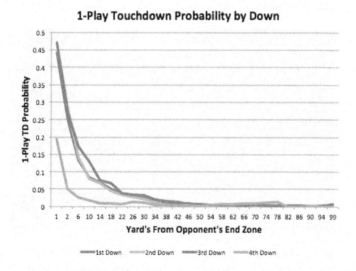

1-Play Touchdown Probability by Down

This resembles the typical exponential growth curve, huh? Offenses have very little shot of scoring a touchdown from their own territory; 50-plus-yard touchdowns are very rare. As an offense approaches the opponent's 30-yard line, though, things start to look up. We see steady growth until the red zone, when exponential growth occurs.

The conclusion here is obvious: target players who excel in the red zone. I've written extensively on this subject in regards to every position, and there are so many reasons that you need to be concerned about scoring. For one, touchdowns are clearly important. Too important, actually, as they're weighted too heavily in fantasy football. Let's exploit that.

Second, red zone play is consistent. It's fairly easy to predict both opportunities (fuck you Michael Bush) and efficiency; the same sorts of players excel again and again in the red zone. For pass-catchers, weight is extremely valuable (even more so than height):

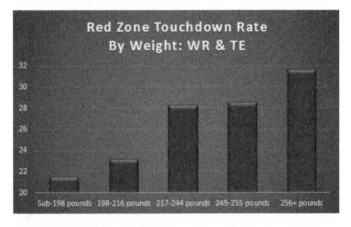

Being tall helps receivers in the red zone, but if you think about it, not many passes are jump balls on which being tall and leaping high will be that big of an advantage. But how many times do receivers and tight ends need to use their bodies to fight off defenders? Weight and strength matter for receivers in the red zone.

For running backs, we want either weight or quickness.

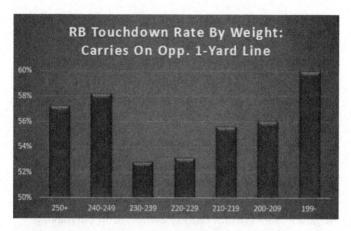

The most successful red zone backs have either had the power (and size) to plow through defenders or the quickness (and usually a lack of size) to make one cut and get into the end zone. Of course, coaches typically play the big boys in goal line situations, so their bulk numbers win out.

As a final note on the importance of touchdowns and red zone play, consider the fantasy scoring on a typical drive. Fantasy point scoring itself is linear, up to a point. If you have a running back who sees every carry on a 62-yard scoring drive, he might accumulate 6.1 fantasy points for rushing 61 yards, all the way up to the opponent's one-yard line. If he takes that final play in for the score, we see an explosive growth in scoring that's completely disproportionate; the running back totals the same 6.1 fantasy points for that one-yard touchdown as he did for the 61 prior rushing yards. We see linear and then explosive growth with fantasy points, and exponential growth in regards to the probability of scoring a touchdown.

Pairing Teammates

If you play daily fantasy football on a site like DraftKings or FanDuel, you're very familiar with the concept of pairing teammates—sometimes referred to as 'stacking'—in a manner that can alter the way you accumulate fantasy points.

In my opinion, fantasy football is becoming less and less about individual players and their projections and more about position types and roster construction. Since projections are becoming more accurate every year, the biggest advantages for fantasy owners aren't in making more accurate projections than the next guy, but in selecting the right types of players and pairing them in a way that can increase either upside or floor production.

Take pairing a quarterback and one or more of his wide receivers, for example. This is a popular strategy in large daily fantasy football leagues because you need upside, but it's not as popular in season-long fantasy leagues because there's a lower floor on production. Head-to-head season-long leagues in particular necessitate a cautious approach each week, and pairing a quarterback with his receivers can be volatile; their play is related, so if one has a poor game, chances are the other one will as well.

However, pairing teammates together creates an opportunity for explosive jumps in fantasy production. Scoring seven fantasy points from your quarterback on a 75-yard touchdown pass is nice, but totaling 21.5 fantasy points on that same play because you had the receiver who caught the touchdown is even better.

The question is whether or not the upside makes up for the downside. In most cases, I'm not sure that's the case. I have some data suggesting that stacking a quarterback with his receiver is riskier than you might think.

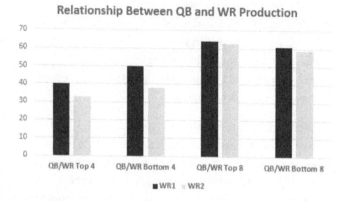

This graph analyzes the probability of either a No. 1 wide receiver or a No. 2 wide receiver turning in a top four/eight performance on the season (in terms of their individual games) given that their quarterback did the same.

So take a quarterback's top four fantasy games; what are the chances his wide receiver also had a top four fantasy game? The answer is 40 percent for WR1s and 33 percent for WR2s. That's above the 25 percent expectation we'd have if things were totally random.

But look at the graphs for the "bottom four" games. When a quarterback turns in one of his worst four performances of the year, there's a 50 percent chance that his No. 1 wide receiver did the same and a 38 percent chance that his No. 2 wide receiver had one of his worst four games of the year—above the "top four" percentages. Things even out when we analyze "top eight" games, but in terms of real ceiling and floor production—the best and worst games of that player's season—there's a low floor on QB-WR pairs (especially for the No. 1 wide receiver).

However, there are a couple reasons I'd still consider drafting a quarterback and wide receiver pair in season-long formats. The first is that it's not like you don't need upside at all in a head-to-head league. You're still competing against 11 other owners in most leagues, so you need to take some chances.

The second is that there are certain quarterback/wide receiver pairs that are probably less susceptible to wild swings in production. WR1s who have elite wide receivers opposite them, for example, typically 1) don't see as much defensive attention and 2) don't see as high of a number of targets as the Megatron-esque true WR1s. That means that the quarterback is less dependent on them for his production, and the two aren't so closely linked.

Shootouts

In early October of 2013, Tony Romo turned in one of the best games of his career—and really one of the top games for any quarterback ever. On just 36 attempts, Romo threw for 506 yards, five touchdowns, and one pick. The fact that he was so efficient with over 500 passing yards is remarkable.

And he lost.

On the other side of the field stood Peyton Manning, whose 412 passing yards, four touchdowns, and one interception weren't so shabby himself. Together, the duo passed for over 900 yards and nine touchdowns, each feeding off of the other's performance throughout the game. The Cowboys and Broncos scored on nearly every possession, causing the coaches to continue to dial up pass after pass in an effort to keep up. The fantasy production in the legendary 51-48 contest was unheard of; three Dallas receivers had at least 100 yards and a touchdown, while five Denver receivers caught at least five passes.

One of the ways to enhance the odds of exponential fantasy production is to start players in games that are likely to become high-scoring shootouts with a close final score. The key isn't only that there's going to be a lot of points, but also that the game remains close so that each team keeps throwing. You can use the Vegas lines to easily and accurately predict final scores.

If possible, you want to target players facing an opponent that's going to pass the ball a lot. One of the hidden benefits of seeing the opposition throw is that it increases the total number of plays in a game since the clock stops with incompletions. So if you have a quarterback in a game in which his team is projected to score 34 points and the opposition is projected at 28 points, that's a whole lot better of a situation than one with a 34-14 projected score. In the latter scenario, there's a good chance your quarterback will stop passing in the fourth quarter.

Another popular strategy is to target good quarterbacks who are actually projected to lose in a given game, but that strategy can be problematic. The main benefit of seeing your quarterback get down in a game is that he should rack up a high number of attempts, which is awesome. But if he's down by too much, the opponent will run out the clock, which will ultimately limit the total number of plays for both teams.

That's something many fantasy owners forget; the opponent's offensive play-calling is important to your player's production. Very important. All other things equal, you want to start guys facing teams that extend the game as much as possible and increase the total number of plays for both squads. If you're starting a quarterback playing against a shitty team that runs the ball a lot, he might have good efficiency, but he's probably not going to rack up a lot of attempts because 1) his team will gain a lead and 2) the other team's play-calling will prohibit a large number of total plays in the game.

If the goal is exponential growth, we're seeking lots of passing, lots of scoring, and a close contest.

17 How can I make better predictions?

Nate Silver's site FiveThirtyEight recently launched and there's a really interesting article on March Madness brackets and the difference between accuracy and skill in prediction.

> In 1884, a scientist named John Park Finley set the standard for being accurate but not skillful in his predictions. Over three months, Finley predicted whether the atmospheric conditions in the U.S. were favorable or unfavorable for tornadoes over the next eight hours, and then compared whether his prediction was accurate. By the end, Finley had made 2,806 predictions and 2,708 of them proved accurate, for a success rate of 96.5 percent. Not bad. But two months later, another scientist pointed out that if Finley had just said that there wouldn't have been a tornado every eight hours, he would have been right 98.1 percent of the time. In forecasting, accuracy isn't enough. Being a good forecaster means anticipating the future better than if you had just relied on a naive prediction.

This same idea has an impact on how we approach fantasy football. Namely, we need to be less concerned with our rates of accuracy and more concerned about how our accuracy measures up to what should be expected. A 25 percent hit rate on a late-round pick might be good; for a first-rounder, not so much.

I'm going to give two examples showing how humans are really poor at understanding stats and, in most cases, can be beaten by very simple rules-of-thumb when making predictions.

Let's go back to the NCAA tournament. When I was in high school, a lot of my friends would get on me because I picked almost all of the favorites in our March Madness pool every year. "You're an idiot, a 12-seed always beats a 5-seed."

There were probably 50-plus students in this pool every year and I won two of my four years in high school, but my reputation was that of someone afraid to take risks. In actuality, I'm pretty strongly risk-seeking, but only when that risk is accompanied by upside (and the upside outweighs the risk relative to the probability of good/bad things occurring). But when the risk comes with no upside—as in aimlessly and arbitrarily choosing a 12-seed to beat a 5-seed—yeah, I'm not going to take a needless risk.

The problem comes in falsely believing that greater accuracy is always achieved through greater skill. Knowledge equals power, but more knowledge doesn't always equate to more power. Put my March Madness brackets next to 100 ESPN experts, and I'll probably beat the majority of them with no knowledge of NCAA basketball whatsoever, just picking mainly favorites and throwing in a little game theory.

The question people should be asking themselves whenever they're dealing with predictions isn't just "what is the probability of X occurring?" but also "what's my probability of correctly predicting X?" When it comes to a 12-seed beating a 5-seed, yes, that will probably happen in a given year, but only because there are four such games. The 5-seed will always be favored to win the game, and the chances of you predicting a 5-seed to lose, then have it happen as you predicted, are smaller than the chances of every 5-seed winning.

Let's look at it another way. Instead of asking if a 5-seed will lose, ask yourself which possible combination of wins/losses in the four games is the most probable. Here's how the breakdown of outcomes for the No. 5 seeds can look in a given year: WWWW, WWWL, WWLW, WLWW, LWWW, WWLL, WLWL, LWWL, WLLW, LWLW, LWLW, LLWW, WLLL, LWLL, LLWL, LLLW, LLLL.

Now let's assume that each No. 5 seed has an 80 percent chance to win. What are the chances that all four win? Just under 41 percent. That's less than a coin flip, meaning odds are one will lose.

But it's still the most likely individual outcome. Even if we assume that only one 12-seed can win—so it's either none or one—the remaining 59 percent would be split among four scenarios: WWWL, WWLW, WLWW, and LWWW. So if the probability of each 5-seed winning is 80 percent, chances are one will lose. But the odds of none losing (41 percent) are significantly higher than the probability of one losing *and* you picking that loser (14.8 percent). By arbitrarily picking low seeds to beat high seeds in the NCAA tournament, you're drastically cutting into your odds of winning.

Another example: "at least six new teams make the playoffs every year." That idea leads people to remove playoff-caliber teams in favor of shitty ones just to make sure there's enough turnover in their playoff predictions. But they're forgetting they not only need to predict how many of the same teams will make the postseason, but also which teams will be replaced, and by whom. That prediction becomes way, way more difficult.

If you're projecting playoff teams, you shouldn't just blindly copy what happened the previous year because the best teams don't always make it. But you shouldn't remove a certain number of teams, either; just pick the six best teams from each conference, because that's the individual path most likely to occur.

Finding the Exception

I read a really well-written piece by Shawn Siegele on a similar idea:

> Many people subscribe to the theory that you can't grade a draft for at least three years. This is partially due to the bizarre yet somewhat prevalent theory that it's a scout's job to find the exceptions to the rules instead of finding players who fit the established models of prospects who successfully transition to the NFL. There are two key reasons why it doesn't work to wait three years to see if longshots like Tavon Austin or Marquise Goodwin pay off. First, if you wait that long to self-evaluate, you will make many more mistakes in the interim. Second, it encourages the lottery ticket idea. A lottery ticket purchaser is not vindicated in his strategy simply because a given ticket pays off.

I've always had a problem with grading drafts years after they occur. The NFL draft is governed by probabilities, in which case we can know the quality of the decision immediately. A poker player doesn't assume he made a poor choice because he suffers a bad beat on the river. The decision is either good or bad when it's made, and you live with the results. The same goes for the draft.

Within that excerpt is an interesting phrase: "it's a scout's job to find the exceptions to the rules." That really says a lot about the state of NFL scouting and decision-making. As it stands right now, NFL teams are trying to figure out when they should take the 12-seed to beat the 5-seed. The answer is basically never, but they continue to do it again and again. If NFL scouting could be represented through a March Madness bracket, we'd probably see three 12-seeds moving to the Sweet Sixteen.

Don't be the equivalent of an NFL scout in your fantasy football league. Your job isn't to find exceptions to rules. It's to identify the rules, use them as a foundation to draft, and deviate only when there's a wealth of evidence that you should.

Are you always going to be right? No, just in the same way that we won't always see every 5-seed beat every 12-seed. But as I detailed to start this article, great forecasting isn't only about being accurate, but being more accurate than what we can expect with a simple rule-of-thumb.

In most cases, fantasy owners outsmart themselves. They try to identify situations in which a player or team is going to deviate from what they know is the most likely outcome. Sometimes they'll even be right, just as going all-in with 2-7 off-suit will sometimes result in winning a pot, but that doesn't make the decision the right one.

You can approach fantasy football like your average Joe, making outrageous low-probability picks and rejoicing when one of them manages to hit. Or you can win championships. Your call.

18 Is a No. 2 WR on a good team better than a No.1 on a crappy team?
Data collected by Ian Hartitz

Prior to the 2013 season, I (and a lot of other stat geeks) were unusually high on Eric Decker. Much of the reasoning was based around Decker's size and ability to find the end zone. Dating back to his time at the University of Minnesota, Decker has been one of the most underrated red zone threats in football.

Plus his wife is hot, and I've long been a proponent of drafting wide receivers based on their wife or girlfriend's physical appearance. It's a can't-go-wrong strategy.

Side note: did you guys know Decker and his wife Jessie have a reality show? It's on E!. My girlfriend got me to start watching it, and by that, I mean I found out about it, forced her to watch the first few episodes with me, and now we're hooked. Literally cannot get enough E&J. Granted, I also still watch Real World, so take my TV show recommendations with an entire shaker of salt.

Another reason I liked Decker—as if his wife's looks weren't enough—was that I'm typically pretty bullish on wide receivers who are No. 2 options on their team. When a wide receiver isn't his team's top receiving threat, he drops in fantasy drafts. It's not inherently beneficial to target a No. 2 wide receiver, obviously, but it could potentially be a value situation if such a player falls too far due to a perceived lack of attention in the passing game.

To be clear, I'm not talking about Nate Washington-esque No. 2 receivers. I'm talking about Decker (when in Denver), Alshon Jeffery, etc.—the No. 2 options who play on elite offenses and could easily be No. 1s on different teams. Do high-end No. 2 wide receivers fall too far in fantasy drafts? How much production can be expected from them, and how does it compare to other types of wide receivers? Let's take a look.

The Numbers on High-End No. 2 Wide Receivers

"High-end No. 2." Sounds like one of Kate Middleton's dumps.

To determine the quality of high-end No. 2 wide receivers, I examined the fantasy points scored by No. 2 wide receivers on teams with wide receivers who ranked in the top 10 in fantasy points at the position. So take the top 10 wide receivers in fantasy in a given year, study their teammates, and see how they did.

The main question here is whether or not a top wide receiver helps or hurts the other pass-catchers on his team. One theory suggests that to become a dominant No. 1 wide receiver, a guy needs a certain volume of throws, which eats into the potential production of his teammates. NFL offenses are zero-sum in a way—at least on a per-play basis—because every opportunity for one player is a lost opportunity for another.

The other theory is that all of the things that typically coincide with a wide receiver being a No. 1 option in fantasy football—probably playing on a good offense, likely having a good quarterback, and drawing defensive attention—should also help the No. 2 receiver. So the question is if the probable increased efficiency for a No. 2 receiver on a team with a top 10 player at the position makes up for a workload that's a bit deflated.

If we study No. 2 wide receivers on teams with a top 10 wide receiver—N2WROTWT10WR, if you will—we see that they produce at a higher rate than the typical No. 2 wide receiver.

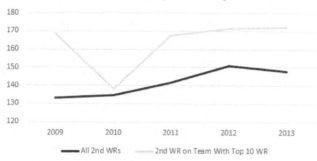

The N2WROTWT10WR (yes I'm actually going to use this ridiculous acronym) outperformed all No. 2 receivers in every season from 2009 to 2013. The average fantasy production for the N2WROTWT10WR was 163.6 points, compared to 141.6 points for the group of all No. 2 receivers. Over the course of 16 games, the typical high-end No. 2 will score 1.4 more fantasy points than the average No. 2 receiver in general, which is significant.

The N2WROTWT10WR don't stack up with No. 1 wide receivers, though.

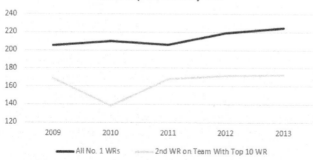

The typical No. 1 wide receiver—remember, that's made up of the 32 receivers who are their team's top receiving options—have scored an average of 213 PPR points per year since 2009. Meanwhile, the N2WROTWT10WR have scored an average of 193 points—20 total points and 1.25 points per game fewer.

So the difference between a typical No. 1 and the N2WROTWT10WR is just over one fantasy point per game, which is also the difference between the N2WROTWT10WR and the average No. 2 wide receiver. But what if we compare the N2WROTWT10WR with only average and low-end No. 1 wide receivers?

Take a look at the high-end No. 2s versus all No. 1 wide receivers ranked outside the top 10.

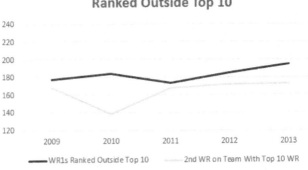

High-End No. 2 WRs vs. No. 1 WRs Ranked Outside Top 10

This is a much closer distribution. The 2010 season was an outlier in which the N2WROTWT10WR performed horribly, but otherwise, they've been very close to producing like No. 1s outside of the top 10. When you break down the numbers further, you see that the N2WROTWT10WR are basically the equivalent of No. 1 wide receivers on poor teams; they probably see fewer targets, but they have superior efficiency.

All About the Draft Position

So should you target low-end No. 1s just as heavily as the N2WROTWT10WR? Probably not. The N2WROTWT10WR likely offers more value because people tend to be scared away by wide receivers who aren't the top option on their own team. Those sorts of players tend to drop in fantasy drafts, while low-end No. 1 wide receivers get overvalued.

Remember that we're not only concerned with production, but also cost. All other things equal, cheaper is better. Let's break this down.

1. Value = Expected Production – Cost

2. Low-End No. 1 wide receivers typically score as many points as the N2WROTWT10WR, but they also cost more.

3. The N2WROTWT10WR will usually offer more value than the bargain bin No. 1 receivers.

A Final Note on WR Age

This isn't entirely related to this lesson, but I wanted to mention that, while going over the numbers from this study, I noticed a difference in age between the average No. 1 wide receiver and the ones finishing in the top 10.

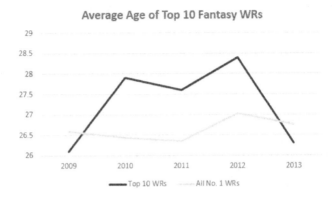

Average Age of Top 10 Fantasy WRs

Top 10 fantasy wide receivers have been significantly older than the average No. 1 wide receiver in three of the past five years, and just barely younger in the other two. The average difference is 0.63 years, with the mean age for top 10 fantasy wide receivers checking in at 27.3 years old.

While I don't think this signifies that "old" wide receivers are better, it does fall in line with the wide receiver aging curve.

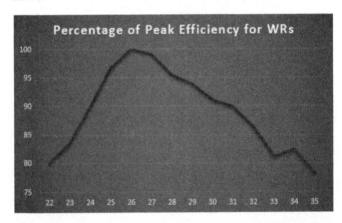

It's rare for young wide receivers to dominate in the NFL like Keenan Allen did in 2013. The rise to greatness is still fairly quick, however, typically occurring within a few seasons in the league, while the fall isn't nearly as rapid. The typical age of peak production for wide receivers is 26 (with 27 right behind), but wide receivers ages 27, 28, 29, 30, and 31 all produce over 90 percent of their previous career peak in efficiency, on average. That's five seasons after the peak at near-peak efficiency, compared to just one before it.

Hence, the fall from grace usually isn't an incredibly quick one for wide receivers like it is for running backs. It's best if the wide receivers on whom you're counting are in the mid to late-20s, but a 30 or even 31-year old is actually more likely to turn in greater efficiency than the youngsters.

19 Are second and third-round rookies undervalued in fantasy football?

Here's my hypothesis: fantasy football owners can get value on rookies who are selected in the second and third rounds of the NFL draft (and sometimes even later). For the most part, rookie fantasy value is more or less a mirror image of NFL draft order. That would be okay if 1) NFL teams were efficient in drafting players and 2) rookies were properly valued in fantasy drafts according to expected production.

Neither is true.

We still see first-round rookies dominate in fantasy football, racking up around two-thirds of all points scored. That's not really all that surprising when you consider that first-round picks receive the most opportunities to make plays. Talent is a big component of NFL success, but opportunity is even greater at some positions, especially in the short-term.

As a whole, first-round picks are obviously more talented than second-round picks, who are in turn more talented than third-rounders, and so on. For our purposes, though, it's not just about talent (and even opportunity), but which group offers the most value in fantasy drafts. We need to be concerned with both production and *cost*. A rookie running back who rushes for 1,000 yards and five touchdowns might be better than a 900/4 running back in a vacuum, but not in reality if the "better" back cost a third-round pick and the latter back cost a 10th. We want lots of production, but we want it as cheaply as possible.

There's something that sounds magical about "first-round draft pick," but there are really just a handful of elite

talents—the Calvin Johnson, A.J. Green-esque players—
who are head-and-shoulders better than the majority of
their draft class. Once you get out of that elite range, the
difference between the players is small; what's the
difference between a player drafted No. 32 overall and
one selected No. 35 overall? Nothing, really, but that first-
round label for the first player is sure to inflate his cost.
Everyone wants first-round players.

So that's basically my thinking behind this initial analysis;
can we find value on mid-round players? I'm going to start
with a quick analysis of running backs because I think
that's the position that's most likely to offer value in the
middle and late rounds.

Rookie Running Back Production By Round

I charted the rushing yards for every rookie running back
drafted in the first three rounds since 2000. Although the
effect isn't that strong, there's still a negative correlation
between draft round and rushing yards, i.e. as draft round
increases, rushing yardage decreases.

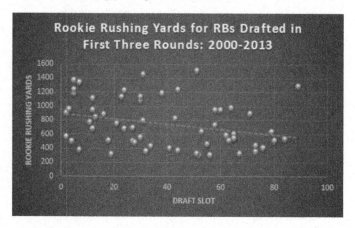

The r-value is -0.28, which is relatively weak. Still, you can see that most 1,000-yard seasons have come from running backs drafts in the first two rounds.

The relationship between draft round and rookie rushing touchdowns is stronger with an r-value of -0.36. All eight of the rookie running backs drafted in the first three rounds to rush for 10 touchdowns were selected within the first 60 picks.

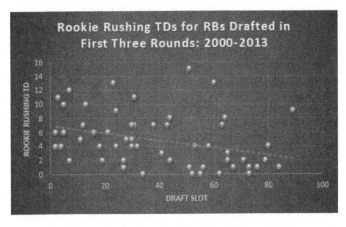

So we know that there's at least some sort of relationship between draft sot and rookie fantasy production for running backs, but again, that's a given due to higher picks receiving more work. Take a look at the trendline for rushing attempts by draft slot.

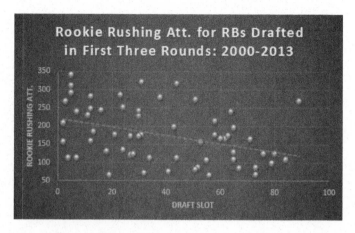

The r-value is -0.37, which is stronger than the correlation coefficient for both rushing yards and touchdowns. That's evidence that much of early-round running back success is coming because of a heavy workload, *not* because of their own talent. It's also evidence that early-round running backs are receiving too many carries relative to second and third-rounders.

To test that idea further, let's examine rookie yards-per-carry by draft slot. Because the correlation for workload is stronger than that for total production, we should see that a running back's draft slot within the first three rounds shouldn't matter much in regards to his efficiency.

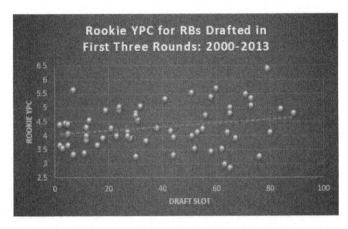

Wow. The trendline is sloping upward, meaning that there's a positive correlation between draft slot and YPC, i.e. running backs drafted later outperformed those drafted earlier. The r-value is 0.22, which is decently strong when you consider it's running counterintuitively to what we'd expect. Due to scouts valuing the wrong traits in running backs and the dependent nature of the position, using draft slot to project YPC is basically impossible. And in any random environment, we should be maximizing opportunities at a low cost. Why pay a lot for something you can possibly get for a little?

Fantasy Applications for RBs

More work needs to be done here to determine the average draft position of rookie running backs according to their NFL draft slot, but we can all pretty much agree that first-rounders as a whole cost more than second-rounders, second more than third, and so on.

Since we know that rookie running back success is due almost entirely to workload—and that the strong relationship between draft slot and a heavy workload can entirely explain the fact that early-round running backs post the best bulk numbers—we can conclude that what we want in a rookie running back is that he's drafted as low as possible while still in line to see a heavy workload.

We saw this in 2013 with St. Louis Rams rookie running back Zac Stacy. A fifth-round pick, Stacy wasn't even drafted in a lot of fantasy leagues. His efficiency was poor, but he still racked up over 1,000 total yards and eight touchdowns, becoming the best rookie running back value due entirely to seeing the workload normally reserved for a first or second-round back.

The key is projecting the workload. Coaches obviously have an incentive to give early-round backs more opportunities; the team drafted them that high for a reason. Workload is such a binary trait, though; we just ask ourselves 'is this running back going to see a No. 1-type workload, yes or no?' If it's yes, we should be living by this general rule-of-thumb: the lower he was selected in the NFL draft, the more likely he is to offer value, and the more heavily I want to target him.

Rookie Quarterback Production

Like with running backs, we see first-round rookie quarterbacks put up the biggest fantasy numbers. The r-value for the correlation between draft slot and rookie passing yards for quarterbacks selected in the first three rounds is -0.29. That's not all that strong, and perhaps already evidence to value second and third-round passers who are starting.

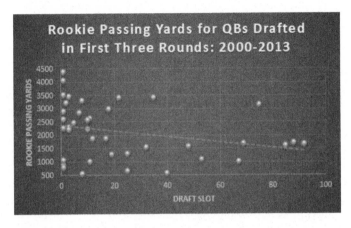

When analyzing passing touchdowns, we see the exact same correlation coefficient of -0.29. Draft slot predicts passing yards and touchdowns equally well.

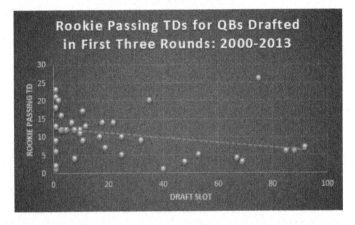

For our purposes, we want to be able to isolate skill from opportunity as much as possible. Opportunities are of course important—crucial—in fantasy football, but we also need to be able to answer the question "If this guy gets playing time, is he going to produce at a high level?"

Answering that question is so vital because it allows for arbitrage situations—scenarios when we can acquire production similar to that of Player X, but at a cheaper price. Quarterbacks selected in the first round of the NFL draft get drafted the highest in fantasy leagues, but how much better are they than second-round rookies who see a similar workload, for example? If the second-rounder can post numbers that are similar, or even slightly worse, he'll probably be a better pick since he won't get drafted nearly as high in your fantasy league.

Isolating QB Talent

Before trying to control the numbers to assess "true" talent, let's look at the effect of workload on rookie passing stats. Check out the distribution of passing attempts (minimum 50) for quarterbacks drafted in the first three rounds.

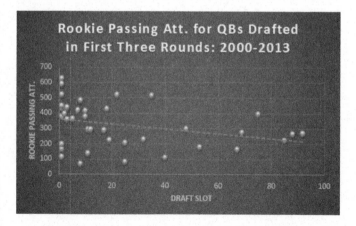

The relationship here is even stronger than that for passing yards and touchdowns with an r-value of -.30. That means that the majority of rookie quarterback success is coming from opportunities, not from efficiency.

If we look at historic yards-per-attempt, we see that it's not at all a strong factor.

That trendline is nearly parallel to the x-axis, meaning there's almost no correlation between YPA and draft slot. The r-value is -0.08, which is very weak. That means that since 2000, there's not too strong of a relationship between draft round and passing efficiency for quarterbacks selected in the first three rounds; a third-round rookie's YPA will usually be very comparable to a first-rounder.

Fantasy Applications for QBs

In the running back analysis, this is what I wrote:

> *More work needs to be done here to determine the average draft position of rookie running backs according to their NFL draft slot, but we can all pretty much agree that first-rounders as a whole cost more than second-rounders, second more than third, and so on.*

Since we know that rookie running back success is due almost entirely to workload—and that the strong relationship between draft slot and a heavy workload can entirely explain the fact that early-round running backs post the best bulk numbers—we can conclude that what we want in a rookie running back is that he's drafted as low as possible while still in line to see a heavy workload.

The key is projecting the workload. Coaches obviously have an incentive to give early-round backs more opportunities; the team drafted them that high for a reason. Workload is such a binary trait, though; we just ask ourselves 'is this running back going to see a No. 1-type workload, yes or no?' If it's yes, we should be living by this general rule-of-thumb: the lower he was selected in the NFL draft, the more likely he is to offer value, and the more heavily I want to target him.

Sub in 'quarterback' for 'running back.' And with that, my work here is finished. Onto the wide receivers.

Rookie Wide Receiver Production

Like with quarterbacks and running backs, there's a negative correlation between draft slot and bulk production for rookie wide receivers. I looked at all wide receivers drafted in the first three rounds since 2000 to record at least 20 receptions in their rookie years.

Why 20? It's a pretty low number that includes the majority of players, but it also assumes at least a low level of usage that I wanted in this study. Remember, I'm not trying to figure out if first-round players are better than third-rounders—we know they are, as a whole—but whether or not rookie fantasy production is due more to workload or talent.

We know lots of third-round rookies in particular aren't going to see a lot of playing time in their first seasons, but we'd also presumably know not to select them high, or at all, in fantasy drafts. Instead of "which player is the best in a vacuum?" we want to know "among the players who will see a workload that could make them fantasy-relevant, which will perform the best?"

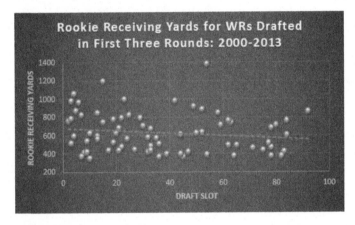

The r-value here is -0.16. That's the weakest of the three positions, by far, suggesting that draft slot isn't quite as important for rookie wide receivers as it is for quarterbacks and running backs, even when we're talking about bulk stats.

We see a similar effect with touchdowns.

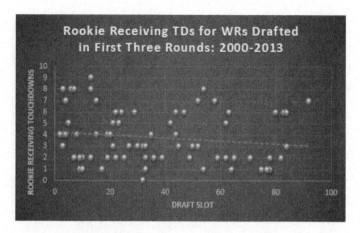

The correlation coefficient for draft slot and rookie touchdowns is -0.15, meaning draft slot predicts receiving touchdowns about equally as well as it predicts receiving yards.

The weak correlations suggest that either coaches are more willing to give playing time to mid-round receivers than mid-round players at other spots, or else teams are just inefficient at valuing wide receiver talent. Knowing how teams have drafted in the past, I'm betting it's primarily the latter.

The wide receiver market has and continues to be horribly inefficient because teams are valuing speed too much and size not enough. That's reflected in the touchdown rate (percentage of catches to go for touchdowns) of this group.

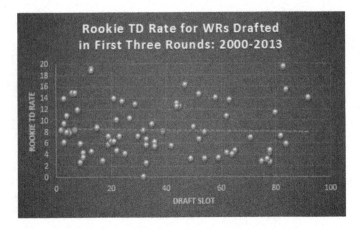

An r-value of -0.04 shows that we basically can't at all predict a rookie wide receiver's touchdown rate using his draft slot; a third-rounder is likely to have as high of a touchdown rate as a first-rounder.

I think touchdown rate is important because 1) a player's ability to find the end zone, though volatile in the short-term, is very consistent over long periods of time and 2) touchdowns are of obvious value in both real and fantasy football.

So again, what we have here is the artificial inflation of bulk stats due to opportunities. First-round quarterbacks, running backs, and wide receivers are all either just slightly more efficient or less efficient than second and third-rounders, but they're drafted much higher.

We need that workload in fantasy football, but even when a mid-round rookie looks like he's going to be the man on his team, he usually gets selected way behind the highly coveted first-rounders. There are all kinds of rookies who are valuable and in no way do I think you should avoid all first-rounders, but in most cases, you can really generate more value by identifying talented second and third-round players who are set to see a first-round workload; you're going to acquire first-round production, or very close to it, at a fraction of the cost.

20 How can I follow the 80-20 rule in fantasy football?

Many of you have probably heard of the Pareto principle, better known as the 80-20 rule. Simply put, the principle suggests that many natural phenomena follow a power law distribution that results in 20 percent of causes producing around 80 percent of effects.

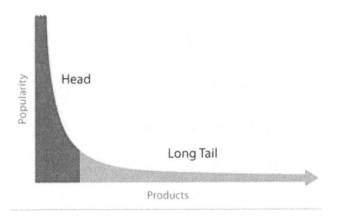

Most companies see that a small percentage of their profits produce the majority of their revenue. I actually see that with my fantasy football books and products; the top 20 percent of them result in roughly 80 percent of my profit. Actually, the top fifth of you guys produce four-fifths of my revenue. So if you're reading this and you know you aren't in that top 20 percent in terms of purchases, get moving.

We see the 80-20 principle in lots of aspects of everyday life; 20 percent of pea pods contain 80 percent of peas, 20 percent of the world holds 80 percent of the wealth, and so on.

The 80-20 rule can have a potentially drastic effect on our fantasy football success. There are all kinds of strategies that fantasy football owners employ that result in almost no benefit, while a few key techniques produce the majority of success. By focusing on the few actions that produce the most beneficial results, we can become far more efficient as fantasy owners.

With that said, I want to take a look at both "the 80" and "the 20."

The 80

By "the 80," I mean the tasks in which fantasy owners typically partake that produce a small percentage of what helps them win. This category could also be called "the inefficient." They're time-suckers; it's not that everything in "the 80" is useless, but we just don't see a very good return on our time.

Re-Watching Games

In the fantasy football world, this is the equivalent of "tape study." You can also throw in long sessions of basically stalking men in their young 20s via their YouTube highlights. Former Lions head coach Jim Schwartz said he basically got a boner watching Jahvid Best coming out of college, and I've had my fair share of CPYBs—college prospect YouTube boners.

Watching highlights or even re-watching games is fun, so it's still worthwhile for the entertainment value. But it's not going to be a great source of knowledge, for a few reasons.

First, it's time-consuming as hell. Even if you watch the games on Game Rewind or something where you can fast-forward, you're still taking hours to do something that *might* tell you a few things you couldn't find out by just looking at the box score and some advanced metrics. There are benefits to watching games as a way to "study," yes, but the return on your time is minimal.

Second, it's not like we're trained in the art of film study. What real insights can we gain? Oh wow, he looks fast, I should draft him. Uh oh, he dropped two passes, I better trade him. We basically have no idea what we're viewing, for the most part.

Finally, when we spend our time "breaking down the tape," we just increase the odds that we get fooled by randomness. Let's take red zone efficiency, for example. The difference between a really good receiver (30 percent red zone touchdown rate) and a poor one (15 percent red zone touchdown rate) is substantial over the long run, but pretty indistinguishable over short periods of time.

And no matter how good your memory, you aren't going to be able to recall the red zone efficiency rates of every wide receiver just from watching games. You probably won't even know a single one. You open yourself up to believing what you can recall—usually recent events or specific "big plays" that stand out in your mind. So maybe you'll watch DeSean Jackson catch five touchdowns on five red zone targets over the course of a month, including a couple ridiculous one-handed grabs, and conclude he's the shit in small areas (not to be confused with *taking* shits in small areas, i.e. my worst in-flight nightmare). Except Jackson has converted barely more than 1-in-10 of his career red zone targets into scores—he sucks in the red zone—but it's really difficult to know that just by watching games.

On the show Shark Tank, Dallas Mavericks owner Mark Cuban reiterates that he's looking for an optimal "return on his time." That's what we want, too, and re-watching games doesn't provide it. Note that I don't think watching football in general is useless or that you should ignore the games; you should definitely watch as much as you realistically can, but if you're trying to improve in fantasy football, watching games as a form of "film study" is horribly inefficient.

Reading Almost All Analysis

I'm not trying to make enemies here so I won't name any names, but (and I think you'd agree with this) almost all fantasy football analysis available—especially that for free—is garbage. You're probably going to become a *worse* fantasy football owner by reading the majority of content out there because it's often either misleading or just wrong.

Now, there are some really awesome sites out there, which I'll touch on in a bit, but if you're reading ESPN (okay I named one) for the analysis over the entertainment value, you're doomed.

It's always good to take in other opinions and decide for yourself what's smart and what's not. But that doesn't mean all content should be given the same amount of attention.

Reacting to "News"

"News" is in quotes here because the non-stop flow of information emanating from today's NFL has created a situation where we know way, way too much about players, and almost all of it is worthless. I don't think we're that far away from getting an e-mail update alerting us that Brandon Marshall just masturbated.

"Brandon Marshall Jacks Off in Shower – How It Will Affect His Week 7 Performance"

That's not a world I want to live in. Obviously we need to pay attention to important news—injuries, coaching changes, scheme alterations, etc. But if you're going to update your projections every time a coach says "we want to get this guy more involved," you're going to be wasting a whole lot of time. Most "news" is twisted from a single comment a coach or GM might make without thinking much about it. It means nothing to the team, but now you just dropped Jimmy Graham in your rankings because a bored reporter decided to make something out of nothing regarding his contract situation.

The 20

Now let's take a look at "the 20"—the 20 percent of your actions that produce the majority of the real-world value for your fantasy football team.

Reading Informed Analysis

For every 1,000 pieces of shitty fantasy football content available, there's one piece of awesome, useful, detailed analysis. In season-long leagues, FantasyPros, 4for4, and rotoViz are the crème de la crème. FantasyPros has some of the coolest tools in fantasy football, 4for4 is continually among the most accurate, and rotoViz combines unique apps with great analysis.

For daily fantasy football, RotoGrinders trumps all. If you're new to the game, you can check out a free "university" I run over there called GrindersU. RG just absolutely dominates the competition.

The point here is that research is critical in fantasy football, but you need to find people you can trust. All of the sites mentioned provide awesome analysis that hopefully complements the evergreen stuff I give you in RotoAcademy and my books.

Performing Structured Research/Analytics

I recently published an argument that suggested focusing on the small things can help you understand the big picture. In my opinion, you should spend as much time as you can performing research on things that actually matter in fantasy football. Even if it's as simple as using the Pro Football Reference Game Play Finder to see how certain running backs perform when their teams are leading, the process of conducting research will help shape you into a superior owner.

The broader picture is that analytics/stat analysis is efficient and scalable. It's efficient in that you can "solve" complex problems in the blink of an eye, giving you an amazing return on your time. As mentioned, researching DeSean Jackson's career red zone touchdown rate will give you greater insights into his scoring potential than watching every game he's ever played in search of the same information—and it will take about one-millionth of the time.

Stat analysis is scalable because we can build upon each other's work. If someone does an analysis on a particular running back's third-down ability, I can check their research, question their methods, and so on. But how can we build upon someone else's film study? Just say "nuh-uh"?

Aggregating Rankings

Finally, aggregating data is perhaps the most efficient way to make accurate predictions. Nate Silver aggregates poll results when predicting election outcomes, and I do the same in my fantasy football rankings at Fantasy Football Drafting. I import the projections of experts I trust, aggregate the data, weight it based on their past accuracy, then alter the projections based on traits I think are undervalued by the market, even a market of experts—things like straight-line speed and pass-catching ability for running backs, weight for wide receivers, length for tight ends, hand size and adjusted-YPA for quarterbacks, and so on.

The 20 of the 20

The reason I'm a proponent of intense focus in a limited number of areas—and how that aids in grasping the big picture—is related to the 80-20 rule. Basically, we want to focus on the 20 percent of actions that create the best ROI. But we can basically do that ad infinitum, i.e. focus on "the 20 of the 20"—the top 20 percent of the most productive 20 percent of actions—and then "the 20 of the 20 of the 20," and so on.

It follows that the greatest potential returns are going to come from exhausting value from the most specific of sources. If we're logically breaking down this argument, it might look something like this:

1. If 20 percent of our actions lead to 80 percent of benefits, we should focus on that 20 percent.

2. If focusing on the most beneficial 20 percent of actions can be extended to more specific actions, i.e. "the 20 of the 20," we should do that.

3. The 80-20 rule applies to fantasy football and, in most cases, can indeed be extended indefinitely in that realm.

4. Therefore, we should continue to identify and exploit the most valuable actions we take in fantasy football, and the most valuable aspects of those actions, and the most valuable aspects of *those* actions, and so on, until we extract the maximum value and optimal return on our time. In short, start with the very specific—the big-time ROI actions—and move to the broad as all possible advantages are garnered.

In this argument, we have a sort of "Russian doll" situation; think of the smallest doll as possessing the most value. We want to work our way to that doll, generate the most possible value from it, then move outward to the next-largest doll, followed by the next-largest, and so on.

In regards to fantasy football, it means identifying how your time can be most wisely spent. Perhaps you decide that it's reading informed analysis. Hopefully RotoAcademy and my books are part of that. But if you personally find more actionable content elsewhere, focus on that first.

The goal is to make you think about where the value lies— how you can best spend your valuable time. No matter where that is, focus on aspects of fantasy football that are falsifiable, repeatable, efficient, and scalable. In short, stick with us stat geeks, because we can take you to the Promised Land.

21 Which stats can I use to predict quarterback breakouts?

One of the things we need to do as fantasy owners is separate what's real from what's fake. Sometimes that's really easy to do.

Other times, not so much. One way to separate the real from the ~~gigantic~~ fake is to figure out which stats, measurables, or attributes are predictive of success, and which are just explanatory, i.e. explain past events but don't aid in making more accurate predictions.

The relationship between running and winning in the NFL perfectly displays the difference. Teams that run the ball a lot win more games, but generally not because they run the ball; rather, teams that are already winning late in games run the ball, creating the illusion that offensive balance is valuable. It turns out that running the ball often is correlated with winning, but usually not a cause (rather an effect) of it.

As I've explained in the past, what we're trying to do in fantasy football is find stats that hold two traits: predictive and underutilized. That is, they need to help us make better predictions about players, and they need to not be used by the general public (or else their value will disappear).

A RotoAcademy reader recently contacted me with an idea—use an advanced stat known as "Expected Points Added" (EPA) to potentially predict fantasy football breakouts—along with some data. Developed by Brian Burke of Advanced NFL Stats, EPA is a really cool stat, so I want to let him explain what it is:

> *The value of a football play has traditionally been measured in yards gained. Unfortunately, yards is a flawed measure because not all yards are equal. For example, a 4-yard gain on 3rd down and 3 is much more valuable than a 4-yard gain on 3rd and 8. Any measure of success must consider the down and distance situation.*
>
> *Field position is also an important consideration. Yards gained near the goal line are tougher to come by and are more valuable than yards gained at midfield. Yards lost near one's own goal line can*

be more costly as well.

We can measure the values of situations and, by extension, the outcomes of plays by establishing an equivalence in terms of points. To do this we can start by looking back through recent NFL history at the 'next points scored' for all plays. For example, if we look at all 1st and 10s from an offense's own 20-yard line, the team on offense will score next slightly more often than its opponent. If we add up all the 'next points' scored for and against the offense's team, whether on the current drive or subsequent drives, we can estimate the net point advantage an offense can expect for any football situation. For a 1st and 10 at an offense's own 20, it's +0.4 net points, and at the opponent's 20, it's +4.0 net points. These net point values are called Expected Points (EP), and every down-distance-field position situation has a corresponding EP value.

Suppose the offense has a 1st and 10 at midfield. This situation is worth +2.0 EP. A 5-yard gain would set up a 2nd and 5 from the 45, which corresponds to a +2.1 EP. Therefore, that 5-yard gain in that particular situation represents a +0.1 gain in EP. This gain is called Expected Points Added (EPA). Likewise, a 5-yard loss on 1st down at midfield would create a 2nd and 15 from the offense's own 45. That situation is worth +1.2 EP, representing a net difference of -0.8 EPA.

EPA does an awesome job of adjusting for game situations to capture "true" talent. The question is if we can effectively apply it to fantasy football.

EPA/Play for QBs

To test how much of an impact EPA has on fantasy production, I compared the EPA/play and fantasy points/play (FP/play) generated by the league's top quarterbacks. I thought quarterback would be a good place to start because, by and large, the best fantasy quarterbacks are also the best "real life" quarterbacks—as opposed to a position like running back at which the relationship isn't as strong.

For reference, the top quarterback in EPA/play (among quarterbacks who played in more than eight games) in 2013 was unsurprisingly Peyton Manning. His 0.33 EPA topped Nick Foles and Aaron Rodgers (both 0.28 EPA). That means that on the typical play, Manning was worth 0.33 points to the Broncos, which is pretty insane. The worst quarterback in 2013 was Matt Schaub with an EPA of -0.08, meaning every time he dropped back to pass, he cost the Texans nearly one-tenth of a point.

On the surface, it seems like EPA/play should be a really strong indicator of fantasy production. And if we compare EPA/play and FP/play in a single season, we see the two are ridiculously strongly correlated.

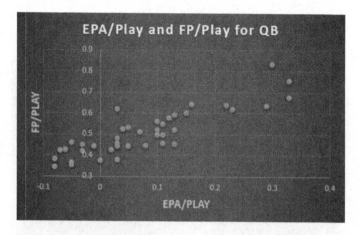

That's basically a straight line, which shows the best quarterbacks in terms of generating expected points for their teams are also the best in fantasy football. The r-value here is 0.87, which is very, very strong.

Just as a reference, I ran the correlation between completion rate and FP/play, and that came out to 0.57—stronger than I thought it would be, but still much weaker than the correlation between EPA and fantasy points.

Now here's the catch. . .

So EPA is really strongly linked to fantasy production in a given year. That's cool—and expected—but can we use EPA/play to predict future fantasy success?

The answer is "I don't think so." Well, that's my answer. Your answer would be "Jonathan Bales doesn't think so, but I have no idea because I've just been thinking EPA stands for Environmental Protection Agency this whole time."

Well, I charted EPA/play in year N versus fantasy points per play in the subsequent season (year N+1).

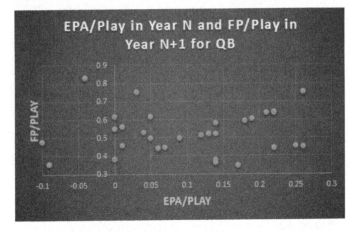

Not so linear anymore. There's barely a relationship here with a strength of correlation of just 0.064. That effectively means that EPA/play is really good at capturing what a particular quarterback has done in the past, but not useful to us in predicting future fantasy output.

I want to note that EPA has all kinds of awesome uses—some of which are predictive in other areas—but it just doesn't appear to be all that useful for fantasy purposes. If you're wondering, completion percentage in year N has a 0.20 correlational strength with fantasy points per play in year N+1; we know that there's a lot more to fantasy quarterback production than completion rate, so that shows just how explanatory EPA is when it comes to fantasy football results.

Adjusted Yards-Per-Attempt
I didn't want to leave this analysis by telling you "Hey, you know this somewhat obscure metric that you almost

certainly never considered using before reading this? Well yeah, continue not giving a shit about it."

So I did some more work to find some numbers that might be of use to you. The first that came to mind in regards to quarterbacks was Adjusted Yards-Per-Attempt (AYPA). AYPA rewards quarterbacks for touchdown passes and penalizes them for interceptions, and it's one of them most predictive stats in all of football. It's cousin— Adjusted Net Yards-Per-Attempt, which factors sacks into the mix as well—is perhaps the only stat that can better predict team wins.

AYPA has a ton of use to those who bet on football games, and it's certainly correlated with fantasy success, too; the r-value for the correlation between AYPA and fantasy points is 0.89—even stronger than that for EPA/play.

But is it a cause of fantasy success, i.e. can we predict future breakouts by analyzing AYPA? Again, Jonathan Bales doesn't think so. The correlation between AYPA in year N and FP/play in year N+1 is 0.078—very weak.

Real Recognize Real

"Real recognize real" is a saying, right? Like I'm not just making that up? I'm not entirely sure what it means, but I'm pretty sure it's applicable here.

Fantasy points predict fantasy points. Metrics like AYPA and EPA/play are important because they show how efficient a quarterback has been—and will likely continue to be in the future—but there's a lot more that goes into being a productive fantasy quarterback. You want efficiency, of course, but you also want lots of attempts, a quality defense to provide good field position, and so on.

The numbers show that the best predictor of FP/play is indeed FP/play; if you want a fantasy quarterback who is going to be productive in the future, pick one who has been productive in the past.

That advice might seem painfully obvious, but I'm not sure that's the case. There are some positions at which past production probably isn't the best way to find value. For example, running backs enter the NFL at peak efficiency.

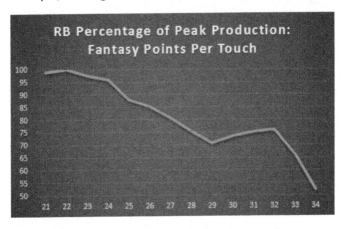

That means when you buy into a running back, he's probably going to be a slightly worse version of what he was in the past, at least in terms of efficiency. That's not true for quarterbacks, who have a much different aging curve.

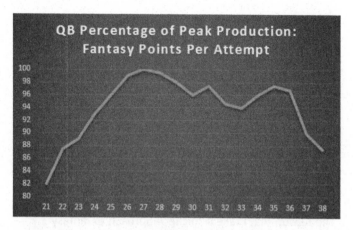

When you buy into a quarterback who has produced in the past, there's a very good chance he'll improve or at least repeat that production again, depending on his age. Explained in the most tautological form possible: if you want a quality fantasy quarterback, pick a quality fantasy quarterback.

FP/play recognize FP/play, motherfucker.

22 Why should I focus on "the little things" in fantasy football?

I write a lot of words on topics that might at times seem trivial. Someone on Twitter messaged me recently and said "Why do you focus on such minor shit? It's useless."

Obviously I disagree that what I do is useless, but I'd have to agree that I tend to harp on traits or events that, in certain contexts, can be deemed as "minor." But there's a method to my madness.

The reason that I take a "niche" approach to fantasy football is because I believe that the sum of those minor advantages—many of which can be acquired with a very small return on my time—will add up to something large over the course of time.

Here's my attempt to explain why I think that's the case.

Markets Offer Value for Unappreciated Data

I've mentioned that fantasy football is a market in that you compete for assets, driving their cost up or down based on demand. It's very much the same as the stock market. Every stock has value at a certain price (and every stock is also a poor value at a certain point); it's all about a comparison of future production and cost.

That cost is basically based upon public opinion; if Zac Stacy has a career year, he's going to shoot up in price the following season because his demand will be high. Note that, while Stacy's "inherent value"—or his worth independent of his cost—would increase, his *actual* value in fantasy drafts might decrease; it just depends on how high he rises.

When we're trying to find actual value, we're really comparing how "inherent value" matches up with public perception; if the public perception of a player's value is lower than his inherent value, he'll offer actual draft value.

Uncovering inefficiencies in public perception is easier said than done. We know the general public is going to value common stats—like yards and touchdowns—as well as other obvious traits. Those things might be important in projecting a player, but they aren't going to help us obtain actual fantasy football value because they're already priced into a player's draft slot.

Thus, to find usable value, our attention must naturally be skewed to those traits or stats that are unappreciated—often those considered "minor." I focus on the details not only because they're predictive, but because others aren't and it creates a potentially large advantage for me.

An Example of Using the Minor

I have a ton of data showing height and weight are more important than speed for wide receivers. But let's assume that they weren't. Let's assume for a second that size and speed mattered exactly the same for wide receivers. Which one is more useful?

Most would answer that they're equally useful; if they're equally predictive, they must have the same value to teams. That might be true in a vacuum, but the correct answer is that, in a market, the measurable with the most actual value would be the one that's least utilized by others—that is, the trait that isn't completely priced into a wide receiver's draft slot.

In the real world, the public perception of speed is that it's more important than size; teams fall in love with fast wide receivers and completely account for that speed during the draft, sometimes even overdoing it (see Tavon Austin).

Does speed matter for wide receivers? Yeah, of course; it matters for every position, some more than others. The idea here isn't only how predictive speed is for receivers or how much it matters on the field, but rather how fully teams are accounting for it in their actions. And because they really value straight-line speed, you generally can't find value on receivers my emphasizing it, *even though it matters*.

Another example is how teams grade running backs. Emphasizing quickness, many teams are bullish on backs who time well in the short shuttle, even though it's a useless drill for predicting NFL success. While the 40-yard dash is incredibly predictive of NFL success for running backs, the short shuttle has basically zero predictive ability.

But here's where things get a little weird; even though the short shuttle doesn't help identify quality running backs, you should still care about it. How is that possible? Public perception. Since teams value the short shuttle, they'll often draft players they deem as "quick" higher than those with elite straight-line speed. The fantasy owners in your league will follow suit, drafting rookies and other young players in accordance with how they were selected in the actual NFL draft.

Since you know the short shuttle doesn't matter in terms of predicting great running backs but that it's still a component of draft slot, you should purposely seek out backs who dropped because of a lackluster short shuttle (but those who were above-average in the 40-yard dash). Because of how both the NFL draft and fantasy football leagues are set up, there's value in going against the grain. That can mean seeking "underachievers" in areas that don't matter much but are still deemed important by the rest of the market, or by bypassing "overachievers" in areas that the market values too much. No matter what, an understanding of how the market will react to certain stats/measurables/traits is a central component of finding value.

A Big Fish in a Small Pond

In his book *David and Goliath: Underdogs, Misfits, and the Art of Battling Giants,* Malcolm Gladwell suggests that, for a variety of reasons, it's suitable to be a big fish in a small pond than vice versa. This idea is exactly why it's preferable to focus on small, "minor," underappreciated traits.

In effect, we're trying to increase our market share of exploitable advantages by decreasing the number of people with which we need to compete. Something can't be exploitable if it's overvalued by the public, so it follows that it's advantageous to focus on acquiring big pieces of smaller potential advantages—those of which people aren't aware or aren't valuing. Here's a somewhat crude representation of this concept.

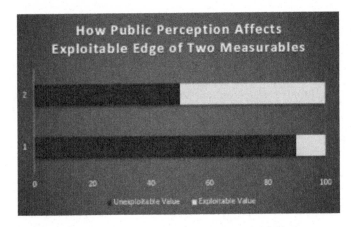

In this graph, the two measurables possess the same predictive value, which I've assigned a hypothetical value of 100. The key here isn't only the predictive capabilities of each trait, however, but also how much they can be exploited. The exploitable value of measurable No. 1 is 90 percent, compared to just 50 percent for measurable No. 2. Measurable No. 1 has more actual value—that's what I've labeled here as 'exploitable value'—because it isn't priced into the market as heavily as measurable No. 2.

Note that measurable No. 2 could be a lot more predictive of success than measurable No. 1, yet still possess less actionable, exploitable value. If the predictive value of measurable No. 2 were 150 instead of 100, the exploitable value would jump to 75—still 50 percent. That exploitable value of 75 would still be less than the 90 for measurable No. 1, however.

Ultimately, we're not looking for the most important traits in some philosophical sense, but just the ones that can lead to the biggest advantage over the field. That's calculated by subtracting public perception—or how strongly a measurable is factored into draft slot—from inherent value (or its predictive ability).

Thus, we get the big-fish-in-a-small-pond effect; by focusing on a bunch of "minor" traits that are highly exploitable, the aggregate advantage can be massive.

Finally, note that some traits can have negative value. If you recall, the short shuttle isn't predictive for running backs, but it's still priced into their cost to some degree. In that case, when we subtract the public perception of the short shuttle's importance (some positive figure) from its inherent value (zero or close to it), we necessarily get a negative number, which informs us that it would be smart to target running backs who have other predictors of success but who struggle in the short shuttle.

Studying Film Is Equivalent to Swimming in a Big Pond

There are all kinds of reasons to buy into the analytics and advanced stats-based approach that I and others are emphasizing; it's scalable, evolutionary, and provides an optimal return on your time.

Compare that to traditional film study—film study that's stripped of analytics, that is—that most NFL teams still use as the backbone of their draft strategy; it's not scalable, it's dogmatic, and it requires a humongous time commitment for relatively little reward.

But there's another reason that advanced stats beat out "turning on the tape." Advanced stats allow you to jump into a smaller pond. If you want to watch a college prospect and try to deduce his NFL future based on game tape alone, you're going to have to compete with roughly one trillion people doing the same thing, including NFL scouts. Even though NFL teams go about drafting players in the wrong way, the scouts are still good at what they do; it might not be terribly useful, but they're still good at it.

That means the exploitable value you can acquire from film study is minimal. So even if an advanced stats-based approach were theoretically less predictive than film study (which isn't the case at all), it would still have more practical, exploitable value because advanced stats aren't a strong component of market prices right now.

Note that you can sub in "traditional stats" for "turning on the tape" and get the same results. If you're going to study solely a wide receiver's yards and touchdowns in college and try to project his NFL future, you'll probably be in just as much trouble; it's not that they don't matter, but that they will already be priced into his draft slot in both the NFL draft and your fantasy league.

A stat like "market share," however, will give you more predictive capabilities, but even more important, it will give you an avenue to accuracy that others aren't utilizing, which increases its value. You'll be able to secure a bigger chunk of exploitable value—swimming in a small pond—to ultimately provide the optimal return on your time as a fantasy owner.

23 Do changes in preseason draft position predict player performance?

Warren Buffett once said "Be fearful when others are greedy and greedy when others are fearful." He also said "Provolone is the most underrated of all the cheeses," and I just simply couldn't disagree more with that statement.

But that first quote, yeah, that one's not bad. Buffett is referring specifically to marketplaces, in which the thoughts and actions of others can and should have a major influence on your own decisions. When others are greedy, it typically inflates perceived worth to such a degree that an asset is no longer of value at its current price. When others are fearful, the exact opposite happens. Simply put, people overreact to good and bad news.

Well, fantasy football is very much a marketplace, whether you participate in snake drafts or auctions. In the former, a player's cost is his draft slot, which we can estimate before the draft using average draft position (ADP) data. It's obviously advantageous to draft players whose ADP is too low relative to their expected production.

I've long wondered whether or not simple changes in ADP could potentially predict player breakouts (or busts). Namely, can we use ADP to identify when others are overly greedy and fearful? When they're too fearful, it could possibly result in a needless drop in ADP, and thus value.

So I checked if that's true.

Do ADP fallers offer value?

Using ADP data from My Fantasy League, I charted the draft position and final rank for players drafted in the top 75 picks. I collected two ADP figures for each player: their ADP on June 1 and their ADP on August 25. That way, I could identify which players were falling during the preseason. I removed any player who suffered a serious injury.

Then, I identified which players overachieved—finished with a higher final rank than their ADP. By looking solely at the overachievers, I figured I might see a lot of players who fell a little bit too far prior to the draft.

But I was wrong.

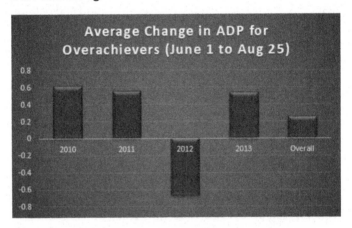

In all but one of the seasons I studied, the players who outperformed their draft slot actually rose up draft boards during the summer. The average movement was just 0.26 spots upward; that's hardly significant in either direction, but it could suggest that blindly targeting players whose ADP declines during the summer might not be such a smart idea.

In addition to the average rise or fall, I also checked the percentage of overachievers to fall in ADP over the summer. Over the four-year period I analyzed, the tally was 51.5 percent.

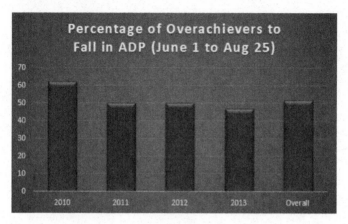

The numbers are a little inflated from a 2010 season in which a lot of players who outperformed their draft slots were fallers in ADP. Still, there doesn't appear to be a significant effect here.

The fantasy football market is far from efficient. There are inefficiencies all over the place that you can exploit; rookie running backs are undervalued, rookie wide receivers are overvalued, and most owners mistakenly take a "balanced" approach to roster construction, for example. But in regards to identifying value based on ADP changes, I can't find any evidence that there's a particular path to follow.

That doesn't mean that there aren't times when individual players fall too far because of an overreaction to bad news. You need to take each situation on a case-by-case basis, but blindly searching for ADP fallers probably isn't going to work in the long run.

There's one specific type of fall in ADP that I believe always offers value, however.

One Type of Fear to Always Embrace

When I hyped up Josh Gordon and Justin Blackmon prior to the 2013 season, a big part of it was because they were ultra-talented players entering their second seasons—a time when receivers typically offer fantasy owners the most bang for their buck.

But another huge aspect of my bullishness on Gordon and Blackmon was due to the duo being suspended early in the year. Yes, I specifically targeted two players who I knew were going to be out for two and four games respectively to begin the season.

The reason is that there's mathematical proof that fantasy owners overreact to the *known* downside that comes with a suspension. That's actually in opposition to how owners treat players who are actually much riskier, but whose risks are unknown.

In an article I wrote before the 2013 season, I discussed why I was targeting Gordon and Blackmon:

> *If you haven't noticed, the rotoViz staff is contrarian as hell. If you think something, we probably believe the opposite. There's a method to the madness, though; when a piece of information becomes popular knowledge, it gets priced into a player's ADP. So I might really like third year receivers coming off of 10-touchdown seasons, but guess what? So does everyone else.*

That's why we're so often looking for predictors of success—traits or stats that typically come before players' breakouts. That way, we can acquire all kinds of value without paying too much for it. Otherwise, it really doesn't matter how much a stat "matters" in terms of scoring you points; everyone values yards and touchdowns, so you can't really gain much of an advantage by seeking solely bulk stats in your drafts.

In many ways, you're like a trader searching to buy low on underperforming stocks, knowing they'll eventually rise in value if they're meant to do so. Well, there are two particular wide receivers—a pair of players who admittedly don't have the cleanest histories off of the field—who are dropping like flies in fantasy football drafts: Josh Gordon and Justin Blackmon, both of whom are worthy of your attention as "buy low stocks."

Gordon, recently suspended for two games, is just seeing his ADP drop as we speak.

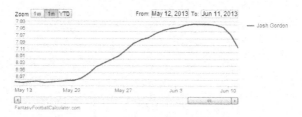

He's dropped just over half of a round since news broke about his suspension, but he's likely to fall even more. Looking back at Justin Blackmon's ADP, we see that it took around a week after his suspension for his perceived value to level out.

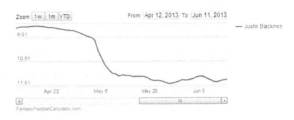

Based on Blackmon's drop, there's a good chance
that Gordon falls well into the eighth round (or
lower). In that range, he'd be the 38th wide
receiver off of the board in standard drafts—down
from No. 30. Blackmon, who once sat as high as
the 36th wide receiver, is now getting drafted at
No. 46 near the back of the 10th round. The
question is whether or not there's value in jumping
on these receivers whose perceived worth is at its
lowest point.

Overall Production Versus Replacement Production

One of the reasons I like to grab suspended players
is that most owners seem to rank them according
to their adjusted overall projected points when
they should be concerned with points per game.
It's not like you can't start anyone in the place of a
suspended player; you get the points for a
replacement player. So Gordon's "real" 2013
projection is (Projected PPG * 14) + (Replacement
Player Projected PPG * 2). Blackmon's is (Projected
PPG *12) + (Replacement Player Projected PPG *
4).

Projecting Gordon Post-Suspension

Looking back at last year's fantasy results, we can project Gordon's would-be full-season production. Gordon, once considered the No. 30 wide receiver, would have probably scored around 118 points had he not been suspended and perfectly lived up to his ADP—the total points scored by last year's No. 30-ranked receiver. That's 7.4 fantasy PPG in standard leagues.

The key to accurately projecting Gordon post-suspension is determining a realistic replacement for the first two weeks of the season. If you're drafting Gordon as the 38th receiver off of the board, he's probably only your third or fourth option. The nature of your draft will dictate how long you wait on selecting his replacement, but if you wait two full rounds, you're looking at the 47th receiver off of the board. Last year, that player scored 96 points (6.0 PPG).

With those numbers, it's easy to project Gordon.

(Projected PPG * 14) + (Replacement Projected PPG * 2) = (7.4 * 14) + (6.0 * 2) = 115.6 points

If Gordon had scored 116 points in 2012, he would have ranked as the No. 32 overall receiver. Thus, taking his two-game suspension into account, Gordon's ADP should drop from No. 29 to No. 32—just three spots—not all the way down into the late-30s. When you consider that many experts saw Gordon as excellent value to start with—I have him in my top 20—it's probable that he's a steal after the first 30 or so receivers are taken.

Projecting Blackmon Post-Suspension

Once the No. 36 overall receiver, Blackmon's projection based on last year's results should have been in the range of 111 points in standard leagues—6.9 PPG. If you again wait two full rounds after selecting Blackmon to get another wideout, you'll be drafting right around the 55th receiver off of the board. Last year, that player scored 85 points—5.3 PPG. That means Blackmon's post-suspension projection is as follows:

(Projected PPG *12) + (Replacement Projected PPG * 4) = (6.9 * 12) + (5.3 * 4) = 104.0 points

If Blackmon falls in that range in 2013, he'll rank as right around the No. 42 overall receiver. Based on his four-game suspension, Blackmon probably should have dropped around six spots among receivers, meaning he's also good value as the 46th receiver off of the board. And like Gordon, many experts considered Blackmon to be solid value at his pre-suspension ADP anyway.

The math shows that, unless you're overly down on a player you know will miss a few games (due to either suspension or injury) for reasons *not related* to that missed time, you should probably target him. The crowd severely overreacts to a player missing games, even though the extent of the downside is understood and the negative impact can be minimized with solid drafting.

As it turned out with Gordon and Blackmon, one had an unbelievable season, leading many owners to championships, and the other was averaging 7.3 catches for 104 yards per game before getting re-suspended for the entire year. That was a bit of a fluke situation, but no owner would complain about having both Gordon and Blackmon on his team in 2013.

The numbers indicate that there might not be value in blindly selecting players due solely to a drop in ADP (without any other context). When players drop because of a known negative—such as a suspension—however, you can easily calculate if that player offers value at his reduced cost. Because of the tendency of fantasy owners to treat questionable players with *known* downside the same as red flags with *unknown* consequences, the former sorts of players are almost always underpriced.

24 Do most running backs fully recover from ACL tears?

Data provided by Ian Hartitz

Adrian Peterson is good at football. It's that type of insight that makes purchasing my content worth it. Hard-hitting analysis.

But guys, Adrian Peterson is *really* good. In 2011, AP went down in the 12th game of the year with a season-ending knee tear. At age 26, Peterson was right in the zone for peak running back bulk production, so the smart money was on him seeing a serious drop in efficiency in 2012, a year older and coming off of knee surgery.

So Peterson rushed for over 2,000 yards and averaged 6.0 yards-per-carry.

We've been taught to believe that knee tears—particularly those of the ACL—can be crippling to running backs. More than any other position, running backs need to make sharp cuts many, many times within the course of a game. It's understandable that an injury as devastating as a torn knee would have the potential to seriously derail a back's career.

But what do the stats say?

The Numbers on ACL Tears

I looked at running back ACL tears since 1999 to see how backs have responded in the year after tearing their knee. The numbers show the average stats for the running backs in the year before and the year after the ACL tear.

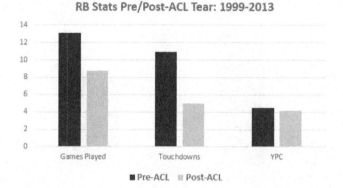

RB Stats Pre/Post-ACL Tear: 1999-2013

One of the issues here is that the sample is already limited, but it's cut down even more because some backs coming off of ACL tears aren't ready by the start of the following season; it all depends on when the injury occurred. At least partially because of that, the average games played by backs coming off of ACL tears is down from the year prior to the injury.

As expected, touchdowns decrease substantially. But take a look at YPC. The gap appears small, but it's actually 4.51 YPC before the injury and 4.17 YPC after it—the difference between a Pro Bowl-caliber running back and one slightly worse than league-average. YPC wouldn't be affected by total games played, so that's a meaningful result.

What we really want to know, though, is whether or not a post-ACL running back is playable in fantasy leagues when he returns to the field, whenever that might be. The most effective way to gauge that is of course total fantasy points per game.

RB Fantasy PPG Pre/Post-ACL Tear: 1999-2013

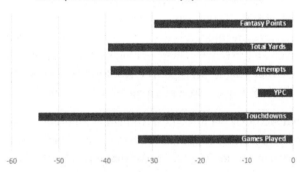

Again, analyzing things on a per-game basis helps control for missed time. And in terms of overall production, it's not even close; the running backs coming off of ACL tears have been significantly worse in their first season back.

Take a look at the percentage drop in running back stats post-ACL.

RB Expected Rate of Decline (%) Post-ACL Tear

The smallest dip appears to be in YPC, but that's a little misleading since there's already such a small deviation in running back efficiency. Remember, the decline we see in post-ACL running back efficiency is equivalent to dropping from an elite back to an average one.

The fantasy points category is again on a per-game basis, and the drop of just under 30 percent is very significant. Since 1999, running backs coming off of ACL surgery have produced right around one-third of the fantasy points on a per-game basis as compared to their pre-ACL selves. That's a serious drop.

Recent Success

There's a general sentiment that running backs coming off of knee tears have been able to return faster and more effectively in recent seasons, due to a combination of superior surgeries and rehab. I think there's probably some merit to that idea. In the past few seasons, we've seen Peterson, Jamaal Charles, and Knowshon Moreno put up top-tier numbers after ACL surgery.

However, we also need to note that there are some unique circumstances surrounding the backs who have rebounded from knee tears in the recent past. In regards to AP, he's just a freak who almost shouldn't even be analyzed alongside other players. He responded from an ACL tear in a way that we've never witnessed and he's so ridiculously talented that we're probably justified in separating the running backs into "human" and "Peterson" categories.

Charles also seemed to defy the odds in 2012, but despite his big numbers, he still regressed from the year prior to the 2011 knee tear; his total yards, touchdowns, and YPC all declined. Still, he produced at a Pro Bowl-caliber level, so we can't really knock him.

The third example—Moreno—didn't actually rebound in the year directly following his ACL tear. In Year N+1, he averaged 3.8 YPC and was pretty awful in Denver. He broke out in Year N+2 (2013), but I'd argue that had far more to do with Peyton Manning than Moreno's ability.

Despite a few success stories, there are also plenty of examples of running backs regressing in a big way following ACL tears: Rashard Mendenhall, Kevin Smith, Ronnie Brown, Deuce McAllister, Edgerrin James, Terrell Davis, Jamal Anderson.

So maybe the rule-of-thumb here is that running backs who aren't once-in-a-generation sort of talents like AP or Charles are probably going to regress significantly following a serious knee surgery. Part of that might be due to the knee itself, and part could be due to changes in usage. It seems like coaches might be a little timid to throw post-ACL running backs into the fire right away, and when they do see the field, it's often in a timeshare situation.

When you combine a reduced workload with evidence of reduced efficiency, you get reduced fantasy production, which is my second-least favorite type of reduction. My least favorite is a red wine reduction. I've just never been able to get into it.

25 How should I draft a kicker?

Your guide to drafting kickers: pick one out of a hat.

Your guide to drafting kickers: let your cat do it.

Your guide to drafting kickers: select the sexiest one.

Your guide to drafting kickers: have a Ouija board?

Your guide to drafting kickers: pick the one you think will be the worst, because fuck it.

These are examples of lines I would have written one year ago. And they still might be mottos I'll live by this year, too. I just imported a whole bunch of kicker data and I'm about to go analyze it. I'm looking for year-to-year consistency.

Why? Well, it doesn't matter how many points we project a player to score if we can't be confident in that prediction. If kickers don't have any consistency from season to season—if we can't use past kicker consistency to predict future kicker consistency—then we could project a kicker anywhere we wanted and it really wouldn't matter. We could multiply that projection by the year-to-year consistency at the position (zero) to uncover the player's value. That's also zero, for those unfamiliar with the concept of zero (I have some ancient Greek readers).

Put another way, imagine that the fantasy football gods contact you and let you know that one kicker is going to score 1,000 fantasy points this season, but every other kicker will score as normal. Assuming you can roster just one kicker, should you draft one earlier than normal? Only if kicker production is consistent from year to year. If it's completely random, it wouldn't at all matter when you draft your kicker; your chances would be just as good in the 20th round as the first.

Like I said, I have the data sitting there—every kicker to attempt at least 20 field goals since 2009—and I'm about to take a look. Be right back.

. . . .

You can't tell but I was working with the data in Excel for the past 30 minutes or so. You might be asking "Why are you telling us this? Can't you just show us the results? Should I pick a kicker higher than normal or not? Are you just taking up space because you don't really have all that much to say about kickers?"

Let's just get to it.

Kicker Consistency

We kind of know that kickers as a whole aren't that consistent from year to year because we have eyes. But are they completely inconsistent? Are fantasy points at the position just totally random?

No.

I charted the correlation coefficient for field goal attempts, field goal percentage, and fantasy points from year to year, starting in 2009-10. When the number is above zero, it means that the kickers who did well in one year also did well in the next. When it's below zero, it means that the kickers who performed the worst actually outperformed the better ones in the subsequent season. The higher the number, the more consistent the stat. R-values under 0.20 are considered very weak.

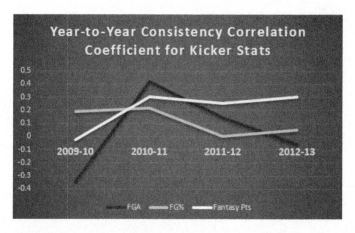

To give you an idea what these numbers mean, consider that all of the skill positions have a year-to-year fantasy point coefficient of between two and three times that of kickers.

You can see that most of the results check in above zero, suggesting that kicker efficiency and production isn't totally random. In most years, the effect is rather weak, but it's still there. The best kickers from one year don't always perform the best in the following season, but it's not like it's a complete crapshoot.

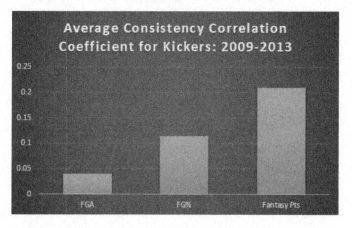

I personally thought that there would be more consistency in field goal attempts than field goal accuracy, but that's not the case. Playing on a team with a quality offense can help a kicker, but it's really difficult to predict how many field goal attempts a kicker will have. The numbers suggest it's nearly impossible, actually.

There's a little more consistency for field goal percentage, but not much. The most accurate kickers in Year N have just a slightly better chance of being the most accurate again in Year N+1 than the least accurate kickers from Year N.

What we really care about is fantasy points, though, and kickers have been much more consistent in that department than field goal attempts or accuracy. The r-value is 0.21. That's relatively weak, but it's strong enough to conclude that kicker fantasy points do indeed carry over at least a little from year to year.

The reason? Presumably extra points. Field goal attempts are kind of tied to the quality of an offense, but kicker fantasy points are very closely linked; every time a kicker scores, it's because his offense put him in position to do so. It's really difficult to predict the touchdown/field goal ratio for offenses—how often they score versus kick a field goal when they enter opponent territory, for example— but much easier to determine which offenses are likely to be good. We want kickers on quality offenses.

Can I take a kicker early?
I made a little kicker flow chart for you to determine your best course of action.

Kicker Flow Chart

Do you have to draft a kicker?

yes → Can you pick up a new kicker each week, if needed?

no → okay so don't

Can you pick up a new kicker each week, if needed?

no → MAYBE you can draft one before the last round

yes → Draft one with a good Week 1 matchup in the last round

What is that a Rembrandt? I'm not one to brag about the quality of my art, but the use of different shapes, the mix of colors, the fact that it looks like it took me 45 seconds to make but was in reality about 20 minutes...just wow. It works.

So here are my thoughts on drafting kickers. If you're drafting on ESPN or some other site where you're basically forced to round out your starting lineup and draft a kicker, then obviously you need to do that. Otherwise, I recommend not drafting a kicker at all and just waiting until before the season starts to pick one up.

The reason for that is because no kicker has upside. When you draft one, you know what position he's in, and that's not going to change (unless it gets worse, like if he gets injured or something). In the place where you'd normally draft a kicker, pick a high-upside running back or wide receiver who could see his projected usage change before the season. If you select a backup running back and the starter goes down during the preseason, for example, you just stole a starting running back in the late rounds. So don't draft a kicker, wait to see what happens with your roster, then get one off of waivers before the season starts (make sure that's allowed, of course).

If you must draft a kicker, the next question to ask is if you have unlimited waiver wire adds during the year. Most leagues allow unlimited transactions, so the value of top kickers is minimized; you can just add a new kicker with a great matchup each week.

What's a "great" matchup? Kicker performances are extremely difficult to predict on a weekly basis, but I tend to just avoid those playing in heavy winds. A kicker playing in a dome is normally a decent choice. Another underrated trait is that the game is projected to be close. When kickers play in games that get out of hand—whether they're on the winning or losing team—their numbers go down because they don't attempt as many field goals. No team is attempting a field goal when down 24-3 in the fourth quarter. So look for good weather in a game projected to be tight—that's it.

If you can't pick up a new kicker each week—meaning you're way more likely to hold onto the one that you draft—then your strategy might change just a bit. In most cases, I still think you should wait until the last round to draft your kicker; most of them are going to be the same.

But what if your top-ranked kicker is available in, say, the 16th round of an 18-round draft? Is there enough position consistency to justify pulling the trigger? In my opinion, the answer is only if there aren't players you like at other positions. If you legitimately feel as though there aren't other options who stand out, then go for it.

But keep in mind that the benefit to drafting a kicker earlier than the last round is small, so you need to *really* not care that much about the other positions. If your top kicker is projected 10 points higher than your second-ranked kicker, for example, the "true" difference is really the projection multiplied by the consistency correlation (0.21), which is just 2.1 points. In effect, you can expect a year-end gain of 2.1 total points by selecting a kicker who is projected 10 points higher than another one.

So in the end, not much has changed at the position. There's a little more consistency there than I imagined, but the replaceability of the position on a week-to-week basis makes it difficult to draft one before the last round. A round earlier won't hurt you much, but don't get carried away. We still aren't all that far from my original advice: pick the kicker you think will be the worst, because fuck it.

Postface

So that's it. If you enjoyed *25 Mysteries Solved to Help You Draft a Better Team*, check out the rest of the *Fantasy Football for Smart People* book series on Amazon or FantasyFootballDrafting.com. At the latter site, I also have draft packages, in-season guides, and individual issues of RotoAcademy—my fantasy football training school.

Speaking of RotoAcademy, the best value is to enroll. You'll get book-length PDFs with written and video content every month, delivered right to your email. Whatever rate you get will be locked in forever (so you'll keep paying the same amount even after the "tuition" increases for new students in the future).

Don't forget that I'm giving away some freebies, too. The first is 10 percent off anything you purchase on my site— all books, all rankings, all draft packages, and even past issues of RotoAcademy. Just go to FantasyFootballDrafting.com and use the code "Smart10" at checkout to get the savings.

The second freebie is an entire issue of RotoAcademy. Go to FantasyFootballDrafting.com for your free issue (RotoAcademy Issue II), add the item to your cart, and enter "RA100" at checkout to get it free of charge.

And lastly, I've partnered with DraftKings to give you a 100 percent deposit bonus when you sign up there to play daily fantasy football. Deposit through one of my links (or use https://www.draftkings.com/r/Bales) to get the bonus, use the "Smart10" code to buy my in-season package at FantasyFootballDrafting.com (complete with DraftKings values all year long), and start cashing in on your hobby.

One reader who purchased my in-season package last year has won $25,000 in multiple daily fantasy leagues.

Thanks so much for your continued interest in the *Fantasy Football for Smart People* series. It's been a joy to write this stuff, especially if it helps you win a league or two this year.

I didn't know that *was* meatloaf.

Sample Lessons from RotoAcademy

Just kidding. That's not really it. Here are a couple lessons from RotoAcademy—my fantasy football training school. I'm telling you...enroll now and I'll give my personal guarantee (Estimated Value: $0.00) you won't be disappointed.

Lesson I: My fantasy quarterback has really big...hands

Jenn Sterger. So sexy, yet so ~~subtle classy~~ nevermind. But she's more than sex appeal, because Jenn—the woman quarterback Brett Favre graced with a photo of his shlong—ultimately led to the creation of this article.

When news broke that Favre won the award for grossest text ever sent, I did what was bound to happen at some point in my life anyway: I Google'd "Brett Favre's dick."

Most of the results were blurred out, but—and this is an open forum so we should just be honest with each other here—that wasn't gonna cut it; Favre's cock was out there on the internet waiting to be seen and, like any red-blooded American man, I knew I had to find it.

I searched day and night. I barely ate or slept, knowing what I had to do. I was on a mission to bring BFD to the people and, after what seemed like weeks but was in all likelihood about 10 minutes, I did, damn it, I did.

When I finally laid eyes on it, only one emotion flowed through me: disappointment. How could Favre, 6'2", 222 pounds, a legend in the NFL, be so...small!? I don't know if I ever specifically thought about BFD before the whole Sterger fiasco (I did), but what I do know is that I never would have guessed it would resemble a baby carrot of flesh resting in his hand. It basically looked like his love line.

HOW COULD THIS BE!? It didn't make any sense. Maybe it really *was* a banana in his pants this entire time. I went for a jog. I took a shower. I paced. I watched Ferris Bueller's Day Off (that's not related but really just a classic).

Then it hit me. Favre's dick isn't small—it's just that his hands are so big. It's a cock-tical illusion!

And could it be that the very trait that led us all to believe that Favre's packing as much heat as a traffic cop is also what made him such a great quarterback? Could big hands lead to passing success?

Let's take a look.

Quarterbacks and Hand Size

Quarterbacks need to be tall. They need to be tall to see over the offensive and defensive lines. If you aren't tall, you're not going to have much of an opportunity to be a championship-caliber quarterback.

That's the popular opinion around the NFL, and I don't buy it. Sure, extra height might help a quarterback in certain situations, up to a point. Given the choice between a 6'5" quarterback and a 6'0" quarterback with all other things being equal or unknown, I'll take the taller one.

But I don't think height matters all that much, and certainly not to the extent that people believe, *even though* I've done studies showing taller quarterbacks have more NFL productivity and efficiency than shorter ones.

How can that be? Well, I believe height is very strongly correlated with a trait that matters quite a bit for NFL quarterbacks—hand size. Tall quarterbacks typically have larger hands than shorter ones; if hand size were really important for passers, we'd expect the tallest ones to perform the best even if height doesn't matter at all.

To test this idea, I charted as many quarterback hand sizes and career NFL stats as I could. I found hand measurements for every quarterback who was drafted since 2008, but before that, it's a crapshoot. Hand sizes weren't recorded well before that time and there's really no reliable source to find that data. Some pre-2008 quarterback hand sizes have been made public in various places, however, so I collected as much information as possible.

To start, I considered only quarterbacks who were drafted from 2008 to 2012 and had their hands measured at the NFL Scouting Combine to be sure everything was standardized. Then, I charted both their approximate value per season (a good measure of their overall productivity) and their completion percentage.

The latter stat is important because I believe larger hands allow quarterbacks to control the football and throw it accurately. If my hypothesis is correct, we should see passers with larger hands have a higher completion percentage.

Comparing hand size with height, here's the difference in the r value (correlation coefficient—the strength of the relationship between x and y) for hand size/height and both AV/season and completion percentage. Basically, I just subtracted the r value for the hand size correlation from that for the height correlation. If hand size is more strongly correlated with NFL quarterback success and accuracy than height, we'd expect the values to be positive.

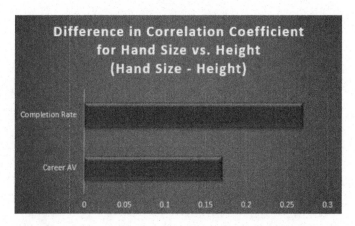

Both values are positive, and it's not even that close. There's a much stronger correlation between hand size and both approximate value and completion rate than there is between height and those stats.

Short Quarterbacks Who Thrive

If hand size really matters more than height for quarterbacks, we'd expect two things to be true: over the long run, 1) tall quarterbacks with abnormally small hands will struggle and 2) short quarterbacks with abnormally large hands will thrive.

Again, that's going to be difficult to prove conclusively because there's not a huge sample of hand measurements pre-2008, but there's plenty of anecdotal evidence that this is the case. Looking back on the short quarterbacks who have excelled in the NFL, many of them have really big hands for their height.

Consider that the NFL average for quarterback hand size is currently 9.6 inches. Well, some of the top "short" quarterbacks (6'2" or shorter) of the past decade have ridiculously large hands—Drew Brees (10.25 inches),

Russell Wilson (10.25 inches), Brett Favre (10.38 inches). There are also countless tall quarterbacks with small hands who were drafted highly and failed to live up to expectations.

Small-Handed Quarterbacks Who Excel

There are some quarterbacks with small hands who have bucked the trend to play well in the NFL, too. But as I studied those quarterbacks, it became clear that the majority have one thing in common—mobility. Some of the top small-handed quarterbacks to play in the past decade include Michael Vick (historically small 8.5-inch hands), Colin Kaepernick (9.13 inches), Robert Griffin III (9.5 inches), Daunte Culpepper (9.5 inches), Aaron Rodgers (9.38 inches), and Tony Romo (8.86 inches).

All of those passers are either runners or have well above-average mobility in the pocket. Romo is the least athletic by far, but even he has been able to work wizardry in the pocket at times to buy time for receivers.

Thus, I think what we're seeing here is that quarterbacks either need to have above-average hand size or above-average mobility to ultimately do what passers need to do to win—deliver the football with accuracy. If you aren't going to be able to stand in the pocket and consistently throw the ball accurately like Peyton Manning, you better be able to move around, buying time to make those throws easier.

When quarterbacks have both traits—like Russell Wilson, for example—it's perhaps a really strong sign that they're going to perform above expectations in the NFL.

Acquiring Value in the Draft

If you talk to NFL quarterbacks, I think most would tell you that they throw through lanes, not over top of the line. Tall quarterbacks have played well not because they can see over players who are often taller than them, but because height is obviously strongly correlated with hand size. Big height, big hands, big accuracy.

You ever throw a small football and notice how much more accuracy and power you can generate? If I could throw with one of those tiny-ass NERF footballs with the tail at the end, I'm pretty sure I'd be an NFL Hall-of-Fame quarterback. Just ridiculously deadly. Quarterbacks with huge hands like Brees and Wilson are playing with the equivalent of a NERF ball.

Both of those quarterbacks are really interesting cases because they fell in the NFL draft—Brees to the second round and Wilson incredibly to the third—because they're short. Brees is 6'0" and Wilson is 5'11".

Somewhat ironically, I think NFL teams (and us fantasy owners) can acquire value by actually targeting quarterbacks who are short but have large hands. They fall too far because teams are emphasizing the wrong trait.

So why not just draft a tall quarterback with large hands? Aren't all 10.25-inch hands the same?

No. Remember, NFL teams are "paying" for height in quarterbacks, so tall quarterbacks with big hands are going to get drafted highly anyway. It's for the wrong reason, but the big hands will still be priced into their draft slot, meaning there's no discount available.

Meanwhile, short quarterbacks with large hands typically offer value because they're being downgraded for a characteristic (height) that probably isn't nearly as important as teams think.

And you know the fantasy owners in your league are drafting rookies based on how they were drafted in the NFL draft, so you too can acquire that same value on short quarterbacks with big hands. If you don't believe me, just compare Wilson's rookie fantasy draft position with Andrew Luck's (or even Ryan Tannehill's).

I actually created a really simple formula to determine how much value a quarterback will likely offer in the draft: HS/H*100 (hand size divided by height multiplied by 100). The higher the result, the more likely the quarterback will be to offer value.

In the 2012 NFL Draft, for example, Tannehill checked in at 76 inches tall with nine-inch hands. His "Jonathan Bales Hand Size and Height Comparison for Quarterbacks Who Can't Pass Good and Who Wanna Learn to Do Other QB Stuff Good Too" value was 9 divided by 76 (0.1184) * 100, or 11.84.

Compare that to Wilson, who was only 71 inches tall with 10.25-inch hands (10.25/71*100 = 14.44). That's just an unbelievable difference, suggesting Wilson was bound to offer far, far more value than Tannehill.

There are more things that go into being a quarterback than hand size, obviously, but when two prospects get drafted near one another, use the formula to see which one was more likely to drop too far, and thus offer value.

Typically, we want quarterbacks who have hands of at least 9.5 inches, but preferably closer to 10 inches. There are of course exceptions to the rule, but the majority of those passers can also beat defenses with their legs. The more mobility a quarterback possesses, the more you can forgive a lack of elite hand size. If a quarterback is a statue in the pocket, he better have some big-ass hands and a history of production in college.

And most important, when a pic of Russell Wilson's D leaks on the internet, don't be surprised if his hands make it look like a Tootsie Roll.

Lesson II: How to Spot a Tight End Who Will Score a Lot of Touchdowns

The tight end position is underutilized in the NFL, particularly near the goal line. As I showed in a previous lesson, there's a ridiculously strong correlation between wide receiver size and red zone production. Well, most tight ends these days are basically just big wide receivers.

I think a lot of NFL teams could maximize their red zone efficiency by removing all receivers under, say, 6'2" and/or 210 pounds, and replacing them with tight ends. To give you an idea of how much better tight ends can be over wide receivers in tight areas, I charted the red zone touchdown rate—the percentage of red zone targets converted into touchdowns—for the top 70 players in red zone targets at both positions since 2000.

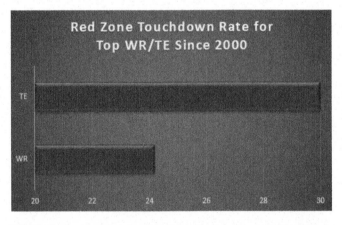

While the best red zone receivers have converted just over 24 percent of their looks into scores, tight ends check in at 30 percent. On any given red zone target since 2000, a tight end has been 24 percent more likely to score than a wide receiver.

Despite that, we still consistently see players like Santana Moss and DeSean Jackson (despite horrific red zone efficiency) playing near the goal line. Nice. Overall, the top 70 red zone receivers since 2000 have seen 6,487 targets inside the opponent's 20-yard line, compared to just 4,202 for tight ends. Those numbers should be reversed.

I've shown that weight is the best predictor of red zone success for wide receivers, with heavy ones checking in above 220 pounds and a few approaching 240 pounds. So how far does the correlation extend? I think it's obvious that extra weight isn't *always* a positive because, at a certain point, it will hinder a player's ability to move athletically and make plays on the ball.

So, let's break down tight end red zone play based on size.

TE Red Zone Efficiency

If you recall from my wide receiver analysis, weight is much more closely linked to red zone efficiency than height. And since wide receivers rarely top even 230 pounds, heavier is pretty much always better. The same goes for height, but to a lesser degree.

Well, there seems to be a pretty linear relationship between height and red zone production for tight ends, too, at least in the height range we observe in the NFL. I broke down every tight end drafted since 2000 to receive at least 20 red zone targets. Here's how they've produced.

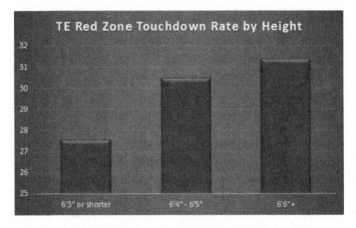

Much like the wide receivers, the tallest tight ends have produced the greatest efficiency. On average, a tight end standing 6'6" or greater has been 13.8 percent more likely than a tight end 6'3" or shorter to take a red zone target into the end zone.

This is interesting because 6'3" is actually fairly tall for a wide receiver. There's really no reason that we should think of wide receivers and tight ends differently, though, at least in regards to their receiving numbers. A 6'4", 235-pound player is a 6'4", 235-pound player; it doesn't matter if we identify him as a wide receiver or as a tight end.

This suggests that although height isn't necessarily as important as weight for pass-catchers in the red zone, more is better. Being in the top-tier of pass-catchers in terms of height isn't a hindrance. There's a really good article at rotoViz on Lions tight end Joseph Fauria, who stands 6'7", which shows he has the potential to be a dominant red zone player.

Note that taller equals better not only in practice, but also seemingly in theory; a hypothetical 7'0" tight end might be completely useless on most areas of the field, but (assuming he's a decent athlete) he could be invaluable near the goal line.

However, the same "more is better" mentality doesn't seem to apply to weight. At a certain point, it just hurts to be a fat ass. There's a reason Joseph Fauria could potentially dominate in the red zone but Haloti Ngata wouldn't, even if he had a normal tight end skill set.

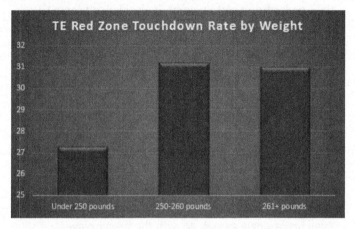

Looking at the numbers, it appears as though more mass equates to better red zone efficiency up until around 260 pounds. That's represented in the graph. It's not like being 265 is a deathblow—you can see that tight ends in that range have still been far more efficient in the red zone than those under 250 pounds—but just that efficiency seems to flatten out.

Also note that if we look at just the heaviest players, we see true red zone dominance. The six heaviest tight ends in this sample have all been second-tier (at best) to below-average players: Bubba Franks, Alge Crumpler, Anthony Becht, Scott Chandler, Jim Kleinsasser, and Brandon Manumaleuna. Hardly a murderer's row of tight ends.

But together, those tight ends converted 110 of their 334 career red zone targets into touchdowns—32.9 percent. That success could very well be due to a small sample size from players without a huge number of red zone targets, which is supported by the fact that those just slightly lighter than them haven't been nearly as efficient.

Still, the point is that even if more weight doesn't help tight ends after a certain point, it also doesn't seem to hurt them, at least in the range observed among NFL tight ends.

Fantasy Implications

To me, the fantasy impact here is pretty obvious: bigger is better for scoring touchdowns. You always have to monitor targets because few tight ends see a wide receiver-esque workload. However, if you're deciding between two pass-catchers who you think will see a similar number of targets (over the course of a season or even just a single game), go with the bigger player, emphasizing weight first, then height.

For example, if I were deciding between a 6'1", 211-pound wide receiver projected to get 110 targets and a 6'4", 223-pound receiver projected at 75 targets, I'd choose the smaller player. You can't make up for that difference in workload.

However, if the larger player were projected at, say, 100 or more targets, I'd be all over him. Even with fewer looks, his red zone efficiency should give him enough upside to make up for a small gap in targets.

The fact that size matters in regards to upside is reflected in daily fantasy football data. In my book Fantasy Football (and Baseball) for Smart People: How to Turn Your Hobby into a Fortune, I broke down winning tournament lineups on DraftKings based on the position used in the flex.

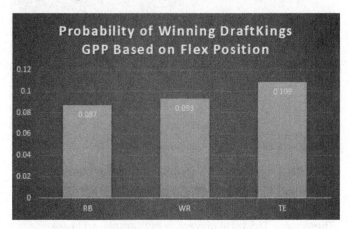

Relative to their cost, tight ends have provided the most upside out of any flex position. Again, wide receivers will normally have better stats because they see more targets, so projecting workload is key. But when the targets are close to one another, whether you're drafting a player or deciding who to start in a given week, you should choose the biggest player, all other things equal.

Comparing Tight Ends to Wide Receivers
Finally, I want to compare tight ends and wide receivers. We already know that heavier receivers are better overall when it comes to scoring, and by a significant margin, but let's take a look at how the relationship between weight and red zone efficiency looks if we bunch all pass-catchers together.

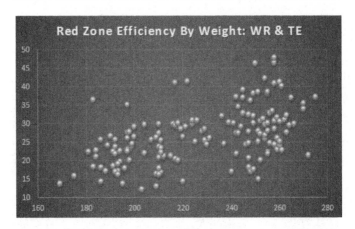

The relationship here is very obvious, with a correlational coefficient of 0.51, i.e. weight is really freaking important to red zone success. Let's break it down into categories. There were 155 total players in my sample, so I broke down the numbers into five groups of 31 players.

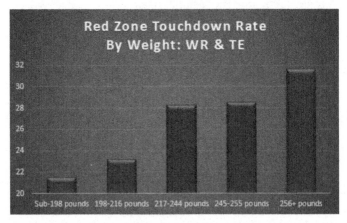

I think I've pretty much made my point here, but I'll leave you with a few player comparisons to show you just how little NFL teams understand the value of size in the red zone.

Despite not playing much early in his career, Wes Welker (189 pounds and 24.1 percent red zone touchdown rate) has as many red zone targets per season as Calvin Johnson (239 pounds and 30.2 percent red zone touchdown rate).

Donald Driver (194 pounds and 19.6 percent red zone touchdown rate) has nearly as many red zone targets per season as Vincent Jackson (241 pounds and 30.1 percent red zone touchdown rate)

And finally, despite never topping 1,000 receiving yards or five touchdowns in 11 NFL seasons, Jabar Gaffney (193 pounds and 17.1 percent red zone touchdown rate) has received only 0.2 red zone targets per year fewer than Vernon Davis (254 pounds and 42.2 percent red zone touchdown rate).

But yeah, let's go ahead and keep Santana Moss on the field inside the opponent's 10-yard line.

CPSIA information can be obtained
at www.ICGtesting.com
Printed in the USA
BVOW03s2137211217
503417BV00001B/58/P